EFL Teachers' Beliefs about Reading and Reading Teaching versus
Actual Practices

Critical New Literacies

THE PRAXIS OF ENGLISH LANGUAGE TEACHING
AND LEARNING (PELT)

Series Editors

Tarquam McKenna (*Emeritus Professor, Victoria University, Australia*)
Mark Vicars (*Victoria University, Australia*)

VOLUME 13

The titles published in this series are listed at *brill.com/cnli*

EFL Teachers' Beliefs about Reading and Reading Teaching versus Actual Practices

A Complex Dynamical System Perspective

By

Yang Gao

BRILL

LEIDEN | BOSTON

This book was supported by the following grants: Dalian Maritime University (grant #02500805), 2019–2022; Central Universities China (grant #3132021330), 2021–2022, the 13th Five-Year Education Planning Project of Liaoning Province (JG20DB053), 2020–2021; Liaoning Provincial Federation Social Science Circles (grant #2022slqnwzzkt-016), 2022; Foreign Language Teaching & Research Committee, China Association of Higher Education (grant #21WYJYZD04), 2021.

All chapters in this book have undergone peer review.

The Library of Congress Cataloging-in-Publication Data is available online at https://catalog.loc.gov

Typeface for the Latin, Greek, and Cyrillic scripts: "Brill". See and download: brill.com/brill-typeface.

ISSN 2542-9396
ISBN 978-90-04-50652-7 (paperback)
ISBN 978-90-04-50653-4 (hardback)
ISBN 978-90-04-50654-1 (e-book)

Contents

Foreword

The relationship between teachers' beliefs and their instructional practices has been the focus of much teacher education research in the past a few decades, in line with the paradigm shift from behaviorism to pragmatism in educational research. This research focus has allowed us to better understand the degree to which teachers consistently and effectively practice their beliefs in their decisions, actions, and innovations in the classroom, which in turn has profound implications for both learning outcomes and teacher development. Filling an important gap in this line of research, Dr. Gao's study provides much-needed analyses of and insights into the relationship between in-service Chinese college-level EFL teachers' beliefs about reading and reading pedagogy and their practices in teaching reading.

The book starts with a comprehensive introduction to the conceptualization, substance, and evaluation of the construct of teacher beliefs, followed by a historical analysis of the paradigm shift in research on teachers' beliefs and practices from a monolingual, positivist one to a multilingual, pragmatist one. Dr. Gao then presents the complex dynamic systems theory (CDST) as a fit theoretical framework for analyzing the systems of teacher beliefs and practices and justifies the adoption of a mixed-methods exploratory sequential design for the study. Using survey data gathered from 96 EFL teachers in three universities in China and classroom observation data gathered from seven focal participants, Dr. Gao systematically identifies the characteristics of the system of Chinese EFL teachers' beliefs about reading and reading pedagogy and analyzes whether and the ways in which the seven focal participants implemented their beliefs in their instructional practices consistently or inconsistently. The personal, institutional, and sociocultural constraints that may have given rise to the inconsistencies observed are rigorously discussed, as are the important theoretical, methodological, and pedagogical implications of the study and its findings.

I applaud Dr. Gao for brilliantly documenting a highly original study in this book, which I trust will make an informative and inspiring read for teacher education and reading researchers, teacher educators, and EFL teachers.

Xiaofei Lu
The Pennsylvania State University
University Park, USA

Acknowledgments

With deepest gratitude and appreciation, I thank those who have supported me in my journey to achieve this book. Without them, this journey would have been impossible. First, I am grateful to my mother. Over the six years of working toward my PhD in the United States and even the recent years I was working frantically as a scholastic returnee in China, I was unable to spend enough time with her. She has been, however, the person and guide who always gives me firm support.

My heartfelt thanks also go to all the members of my PhD dissertation committee. Thanks to Professor William P. Bintz, from my coursework, to the comprehensive exam, to the dissertation and even the book, he has been more than a mentor to me, but more like a father. I also sincerely thank Professors Denise N. Morgan, Sara Rilling, and Alicia Crowe.

I would like to thank my former mentors, friends, colleagues, and all the people who helped me and made things easy for me at Kent State University. Those include Professors Joanne K. Dowdy, Karl W. Kosko, Jim Henderson, Tim Rasinski, and Alexa Sandmann. From different disciplines, they have given me more than just a way to develop my interdisciplinary competence, but also opportunities to practice different research methods.

I also would like to express my sincere thanks to a couple of scholars who are now working in different parts of the world; they either inspired me off campus or set great role models for me along the way I was doing my PhD and completing this book. Those scholars include (but are not limited to) Professor Lu Xiaofei, Dr. Li Shaofeng, Dr. Gao Xuesong, Professor Xu Jinfen, Professor Yan Ming, and Professor Wang Haihua.

My graduate students are also a group of people deserving my heartfelt thanks. It is not only because they helped me with the formatting of the book but also because they helped me realize mentoring is a distressful but rewarding journey. I thus would like to thank Xiaochen Wang, Min Wang, Jintao Shi, Zhaohui Meng, Sen Miao, Tong Guo, Jinyao Li, Mengjiao Ding, and Xiaohan Zhang.

Finally, to myself. With my Taurus stubbornness and persistence, traveling from China to the United States, and then back to China, I achieved my goal and enriched my life. I will keep moving.

Figures and Tables

Figures

Tables

CHAPTER 1

Introduction

1 How the Book Came Out

For a long time I have known that my beliefs and practices as a college teacher exist in a complex manner. This became especially apparent to me when I made my teaching reflection in summer 2013, while teaching a language course to students in China. I took it for granted that the skills I had acquired as a literacy doctoral student and language practitioner and what I had learned about language pedagogy in the United States would benefit my students in China; I thus made attempts to implement different mediators and modalities, including drama, picture books, and movie clips, in that summer classroom. However, it turned out that my actual practice was not so amenable to the students; they were more focused on the test-taking skills, explanations of vocabulary, and grammar analysis and thus did not care how multimodalities and different mediators would work to help them learn. For the very first time, I began to reflect on my beliefs and practices and noticed how factors including different cultures (i.e., American and Chinese ones) and student responses could influence my beliefs and practices. I feel extremely grateful to have had that summer experience, as it kicked off my journey to study language teacher beliefs and practices.

Breen et al. (2001) outlined four points as to why studies on the beliefs of language teachers are important: They (1) enable research to go beyond description toward the understanding and explanation of teacher action; (2) provide insights and reflection for teacher development; (3) align any innovation in teaching practices with the teachers' beliefs; and (4) contribute to language pedagogy by enriching the traditional teaching methodology. These points all resonated with importance through my own story.

Right after that summer, I made it back to the United States, resuming my PhD journey. However, the memory of the teaching experience was in the back of my mind. I had been somewhat shocked by my college students' reaction. I believed, compared to the K-12 students who were strictly test- or exam-driven in the Chinese context, college students would be open to multimodalities and different mediators used in the classroom, willing to give more attention to the learning process rather than just focus on the learning product. However, what I had believed was not the case in the actual classroom. Going a step further, I began to realize that teacher beliefs can appear in different forms

© KONINKLIJKE BRILL NV, LEIDEN, 2022 | DOI: 10.1163/9789004506541_001

to influence teacher practices. Teacher beliefs can appear as an easy-going friend, who firmly supports a teacher's ideas and practices. Teacher beliefs can also be a troublemaker, who causes the teacher to react and change. With that deeper reflection, I dug into my studies on teacher beliefs and practices. With my background working in higher education, I became particularly interested in exploring college language teachers' beliefs and practices. As mentioned earlier, in China, college teachers are supposed to have more wiggle room or autonomy to design and implement their curricula, compared to K-12 teachers. K-12 teachers, aiming to help their students pass the high-stake tests (*gaokao*), have to teach to the tests. In that vein, college teachers are not confined to teaching in this narrow way. As the picture of my study got clearer and clearer, I began to review the literature on the relationship between teacher beliefs and practices.

Numerous studies on the complex relationship between teachers' beliefs and practices have been conducted over the past decades. Shifted paradigms steered educational researchers from a unidirectional emphasis on the relationship between teacher behaviors and student achievements to the correlates of teacher cognition and beliefs with their teaching practices (Fang, 1996; Gao, 2014). As the connection between beliefs and practices plays an important part in guiding teachers to perceive, analyze, and make decisions in class (Clark & Peterson, 1986; Munby, 1982), studies on the topic are very much needed (Farrell & Kun, 2007; Kuzborska, 2011). However, there is a lack of research on related topics and particularly little work has been done on in-service college teachers' beliefs and practices in an English-as-a-foreign-language (EFL) context in higher education (Borg, 2011). One of the important reasons is that we cannot assume even a simple connection between teacher beliefs and practices. Borg (2018, p. 79), by summarizing key findings from the existing literature, argued that teacher beliefs and practices may appear in four primary forms:

1.   Beliefs influence (i.e., are precursors to) practice.
2.   Practice influences beliefs.
3.   Beliefs are disconnected from practices.
4.   Beliefs and practices influence one another reciprocally.

A brief historical analysis helps identify the current state of the study topic. The 1960s through the 1980s was an emerging stage when researchers reached consensus on a unidirectional relationship between teacher behaviors and student achievements; that is, that teachers' beliefs and practices influenced students' academic performance in either a positive or a negative way (e.g., Brown, 1968; Jackson, 1968; Lortie, 1975; McDonald & Elias, 1976; Shulman, 1986).

The 1990s through the 2000s was a developing stage when scholars held two competing views on teacher beliefs and practices (Fang, 1996). One view proposes that there is a consistent relationship between teacher beliefs and practices (e.g., Johnson, 1992, 1994; Kinzer, 1988; Kinzer & Carrick, 1986; Konopak et al., 1994; Leu & Kinzer, 1987), whereas the other view states that the connection between teacher beliefs and instruction is complex (e.g., Ng & Farrell, 2003; Richardson et al., 1991; van der Schaaf et al., 2008). After the 2000s researchers attempted to explore the beliefs and practices of language teachers from a sociocultural perspective, regarding the relationship between teacher beliefs and actual teaching as interactive and complex (e.g., Borg, 2011; Breen et al., 2001; Farrell & Lim, 2005).

In 2016, the Douglas Fir Group (DFG) advanced the scope of studies in second language acquisition, applied linguistics, and TESOL. Among the different fields and subfields affected, teacher education benefited from the theoretical tenets and insights discovered, including the transdisciplinary perspective and the reinterpretation of multilingualism. Thereafter, studies on language teacher beliefs and practices joined other lines of research that were starting to be reinterpreted from the proposed transdisciplinary framework. Tenets from different theories in the DFG, including but not limited to complex dynamic systems theory (CDST) (e.g., Mercer, 2011; Larsen-Freeman, 2019), language socialization (e.g., Duff, 2018), and sociocultural theory (e.g., Johnson, 2006, 2009) all bought great insights to studies on teacher beliefs and practices. Other theories – including translanguaging (e.g., García & Li, 2014) – while not typically covered by the DFG also provided researchers on the topic with energy and encouragement for their inquiry.

In addition to the insights from the DFG transdisciplinary framework, the unbalanced achievements of the existing literature also led us to find a certain gap in studying language teacher beliefs and practices. While numerous studies have been done on teacher beliefs and practices in pre-K-12 settings in the United States (e.g., Davis & Wilson, 1999; Richardson et al., 1991), there is still a dearth of literature on this topic in the EFL context (Borg, 2009; Johnson, 1992). Farrell and Kun (2007) especially noted that more research was needed on the topic as a way to arouse EFL teachers' awareness of how and to what extent their beliefs could be reflected through their classroom practices. Johnson (1994) advocated that EFL teachers do more research to "question those beliefs in the light of what they intellectually know and not simply what they intuitively feel" (p. 439). However, research on Chinese EFL teachers' beliefs and practices is relatively scarce and less developed (Gu, 2017). It dates back only to 2003, when a team of experts in China was formed to work on the topic of Chinese EFL college teachers' practices and professional development, in a national project funded by the Chinese National Research Center for Foreign Language Education (Gu, 2017; Wu, 2005). In the national project, while the topic of teachers' beliefs and practices (particularly regarding the teaching of reading) was mentioned, it was still far less developed (Gu, 2017). The current study thus attempts to focus on the topic and addresses the gap in the professional literature.

2   Purpose and Research Questions

My review of the existing literature on the complex relationships between beliefs and practices inspired me to study EFL teachers' beliefs and practices. In this book, I thus aim at exploring the *characteristics* of Chinese EFL teachers' beliefs and the *relationships* between EFL teachers' stated beliefs and their actual practices. Apart from the characteristics of the Chinese EFL teachers' beliefs, there are two *relationships* to be explored in this study. First, the study investigates whether EFL teachers' stated beliefs about reading are *inconsistently* or *consistently* indicated in their stated beliefs about teaching reading; in other words, whether how they define or perceive *reading* informs how they perceive *teaching reading*. The presence of (in)consistency actually entails certain interactions between the two constructs (beliefs vs. practices).

Second, the study attempts to understand whether EFL teachers' stated beliefs about how they teach English reading are *consistent* with their actual practices in the classrooms. However, exploring the relationships among those studied constructs is not to map out linear, hierarchical, or unidirectional relationships. An analysis of the existing literature and the updated theoretical framework (e.g., Douglas Fir Group, 2016) indicated that the real settings of an ever-changing world have made the relationships more complex. Therefore, through mapping out the nexus of the beliefs and practices, I aim at presenting a complex belief system, especially in regard to how the system may inform EFL teachers' actual practices.

With this in mind, I attempt to address two primary research questions on the *relationship* between beliefs and practices. However, prior to the two *relationship* questions, a question about characteristics of teachers' beliefs was addressed to better understand the studied belief systems. Therefore, three research questions guided this study:

1.   What are the characteristics of Chinese EFL teachers' beliefs about English reading and reading instruction?
2.   Are Chinese EFL teachers' stated beliefs about English reading consistently indicated in their stated beliefs about teaching reading? Or, do

the stated beliefs about reading closely interact with their stated beliefs about teaching reading?

3. Are Chinese EFL teachers' beliefs about reading and teaching reading consistently indicated in their actual practices?

The stated beliefs were solicited in written form through surveys. Survey responses in the written form provided data for Research Questions 1 and 2. Research Question 3 focused on the relationship between the written form (how they think) and the action (how they behave).

3 Rationale and Stages of the Exploratory Sequential Mixed-Methods Design

This study adopted an exploratory sequential design based on mixed-methods design classifications (Creswell et al., 2003). When choosing the research method, I focused on whether the design fit my research questions. Choosing an appropriate mixed-methods design requires the consideration of three issues: *priority, implementation,* and *integration* (Creswell et al., 2003). *Priority* refers to what specific approach – the quantitative or the qualitative – is given more emphasis. Priority is closely connected with the types of research questions – whether researchers want to investigate "what" and "how" in qualitative studies or "if" in quantitative studies. Then, *implementation* determines the sequence of data collection, i.e., whether the quantitative and qualitative data collection and analysis come in sequence or in parallel. *Integration* occurs when researchers strive to mix or connect the data after the data collection in the research process.

The present study is an exploratory sequential design, in that it does show exploratory and sequential features in addressing these issues. For the exploratory feature, the primary purpose (priority) of the study is to explore the relationships (consistent or not), or the interactions (close or not) between beliefs and practices. As for the sequential feature (implementation), it is a multilayered study with qualitative data collected and analyzed first, and then quantified in numeric codes (integration). While the discussion of the study is centered around the possible constraints that caused inconsistencies between beliefs and practices, the exploration of the inconsistencies was the priority. The use of quantitative data in the study was consistent with the sequential exploratory design, in which the quantitative component assists in the interpretation of qualitative findings (Creswell et al., 2003).

The purpose of the study determines the research design and then determines the stages of the study. Therefore, the primary purpose of the study – to

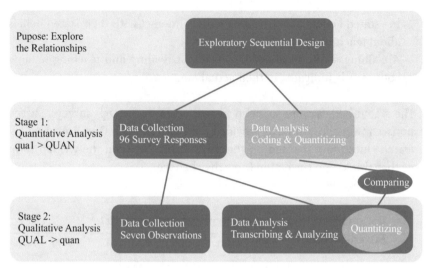

FIGURE 1   Flowchart of the exploratory sequential mixed-methods design

explore the two relationships – leads to two major stages for the study. Morse (1994) diagrammed the exploratory sequential approach as QUAL → quan, which is also the basic diagram for the current study. However, the data collection and analysis process in the study included two subdiagrams/stages. The first diagram was qual → QUAN, with qualitative data being analyzed in a quantitative way, which is termed *quantitizing*. The second diagram was QUAL → quan, with the qualitative description data used to evaluate the (in)consistency between beliefs and practices in specific cases. The following chart describes how the design was structured for the entire study (see Figure 1).

The purpose of the first stage was to explore the first relationship, i.e., the relationship between beliefs about reading and beliefs about teaching reading among the teachers in the study. All the data were collected from the open-ended question surveys, which presented the teachers' responses in a qualitative form. Then, the qualitative data were quantitized in a numeric, quantitative form to confirm or evaluate the relationship. That is the qual → QUAN stage.

The second stage was to explore the relationship between stated beliefs and actual practices. However, instead of including all the subjects from the first stage, the second stage only included seven purposive participants. Qualitative description through the transcription of classroom observations was generated in this stage. Then, the data of the seven participants were compared with their quantitative data in the first stage. That is the stage of QUAL → quan.

The whole process of the study thus includes two major stages in sequence: the first stage aimed at exploring the relationship between two sorts of beliefs, and the second stage evaluated the relationship between beliefs and practices. While the second stage's main purpose was to explore the relationship, it also yielded data to explain the inconsistencies among the different constructs studied.

4 Biographical Information of the Participants in the Book

Participants in the book included 96 university EFL teachers who were faculty members from three different universities in a city in northeastern China. The 96 teacher participants included young and senior faculty members with different years of working experiences, ranging from 2 to 30 years. Teachers of different genders, ages, and races were randomly enrolled. They were categorized as teaching either English-major students (E) or non-English-major students (N) (see Table 1). As the study had a two-stage design, all participants were given the survey to fill in at the beginning of the study, then those who were willing to continue to be participants moved on to the second stage of the study.

The biographical information of the sample is presented in Table 1. Among the 96 teachers who were given questionnaires to fill in, 55 were from the same university, and 18 and 23 were from the other two universities. Sixty of the total 96 teachers were teaching students majoring in English (E), whereas the other 36 were teaching non-English-major (N) students. The gender ratio was approximately 2:1, with the female teachers in the majority. Twenty-five of the 96 teachers who filled in the BRI surveys were willing to participate in the second part of the study, i.e., the qualitative research.

TABLE 1   Biographical information of the sample

Universities	Number	Major taught N/E	Gender F/M	Purposive participants F/M
1	55	55/0	43/12	5/2
2	18	5/13	3/15	N.A.
3	23	0/23	17/6	N.A.
Total	96	60/36	63/33	5/2

Notes: N: non-English major; E: English major
       M: male; F: female

Ultimately, seven participants, all from one of the three universities, were selected for the qualitative part of the study. The seven participants were purposefully selected according to a few criteria, particularly the teachers' willingness to participate, their availability for classroom observation, and the manageability of the study. For example, while the research included 96 participants in the survey part, it was not practical for all 96 teachers to be observed for their actual practices. As the average time for a class observation ranges from 45 to 90 minutes, observations of all the 96 teachers would yield approximately 4,320 to 8,640 minutes of data. It would also have been impossible to gather the data in a reasonable amount of time or to schedule coordination between the researcher and the teachers. The universities would not allow for daily observation, so research would have probably extended beyond a single school year. In addition, the convention in qualitative studies is to focus on certain selected, purposeful participants and yield saturated descriptions of the participants' life experience excerpts (Creswell, 2012). Different researchers in qualitative studies (e.g., Creswell, 2012; Morse, 1994) suggest 5 to 25 as the minimum fit number for participants. Based on the above-mentioned factors and considerations, I finally chose seven participants for the qualitative part of the study.

5   Structure of the Book

In this chapter, I provided a statement of the problem, the purpose of the study, and the research questions. I also described the conceptual framework and then explained the significance of the study. In addition, I provided working definitions of specific terms used in the study. For example, reading beliefs and teaching beliefs that were included in BRI, and behaviorism, cognitivism, and constructivism that were included in the DeFord Theoretical Orientation to Reading Profile (TORP). BRI was used in the study to collect teachers' responses and TORP was used to explain different theoretical orientations indicated in the responses.

In Chapter 2, I review the literature on the topic of teacher beliefs and practices, particularly in the ESL/EFL context. I primarily introduce various definitions of teacher beliefs and summarize the features of teacher beliefs, and then present a review of the existing literature in the field, particularly in the EFL context.

In Chapter 3, I analyze the studies in an emerging stage when researchers had attained consensus on a unidirectional relationship between teacher behaviors and student achievements. I then present a synopsis of the literature at the developing stage when scholars held two competing themes: consistency and inconsistency on teacher beliefs and practices. I summarize the studies after the 2000s, when researchers attempted to explore language teachers' beliefs and practices from a sociocultural perspective and regard the relationship between teacher beliefs and actual teaching as an interactive and complex one. I conclude the chapter with theoretical insights that can be developed and used for the current book.

In Chapter 4, I explain how a pragmatic paradigm worked in the selection of the CDST theoretical framework in the book. I also provide a general picture of why and how CDST was identified as a suitable theoretical framework to use to study teacher belief systems and also their interaction with practices.

In Chapter 5, I describe the research context and sites and give my rationale for choosing a mixed-method design. I also describe the findings of the study which related to the three research questions in this chapter. Generally, in terms of the characteristics in the Chinese teacher belief system, three theoretical orientations to reading coexist: behaviorism, cognitivism, and constructivism. In addition, three distinct theoretical orientations or reading belief systems are identified: dominant, dual, and multiple.

In Chapter 6, I describe the inconsistency among the seven selected teachers who were observed in their classrooms for their actual practice. Only two observed teachers, Y and D, implemented what they believed in the survey in their actual performance in the classrooms. The other teachers, however, showed some inconsistencies between their stated beliefs and their actual practices.

In Chapter 7, I highlight how the book contributed to the current area of EFL teacher education. Findings of the study showed that both consistencies and inconsistencies were revealed with inconsistencies being more prominent. The study also discussed constraints which might cause the inconsistencies between beliefs and practices, including institutional, personal, and sociocultural constraints. The book also offers insights for future studies which could be conducted from an ecological, dynamic perspective. Together with the discussed insights, I propose a model for studying EFL teachers' beliefs and practices.

In Chapter 8, the concluding chapter, I summarize the major points in the book and even in the field, and also provide insights into how scholars may extend the line of inquiry in the future.

The book attempts to make some theoretical contribution in the way that CDST has been adopted and adapted to the studies on EFL teachers' beliefs and practices. Studies over the decades have provided the field with an influx of theoretical frameworks, particularly from the cognitive sciences, psychological studies, and educational or learning theories. The latest research paradigm pragmatism has yielded great insights to explore the complex, ever-changing world from a multidimensional, dynamic perspective. We have thus gone through the linguistic turn, the sociocultural turn (Johnson, 2006), to the most recent multilingual turn (García & Li, 2014). It is therefore necessary to adopt a suitable theoretical framework in the current era. Complex theory caters to the needs and research paradigm and has become a popular (albeit underdeveloped) theoretical framework for educational and social science studies, including teacher education and teacher belief studies (e.g., Martin et al., 2020; Zheng, 2013a, 2013b, 2015). The book joins the new paradigm and adapts the theoretical framework to study teacher beliefs and practices.

In addition, the book attempts to help teacher educators, school administrators, and policy makers reflect on the improvement of teacher education programs or initiatives. The increasing amount of developed technology and content area knowledge has to a large extent facilitated our education, including teacher education. Most teacher educators or school policy makers believe sufficient instructional resources, timely teaching training, or well-planned teacher development programs should equip our teachers with tactics and strategies to teach as we believe and expect. However, in the real setting of the actual classroom, teachers are still faced with dilemmas when their beliefs fail to conform with their practice. Therefore, this book attempts to address this gap by providing teacher educators, school administrators, and policy makers with room to reflect on the improvement of teacher education programs or initiatives.

References

Borg, S. (2011). The impact of in-service education on language teachers' beliefs. *System, 39*(3), 370–380.

Borg, S. (2018). Evaluating the impact of professional development. *RELC Journal, 49*(2), 195–216. https://doi.org/10.1177/0033688218784371

Breen, M. P., Hird, B., Milton, M., Oliver, R., & Thwaite, A. (2001). Making sense of language teaching: Teachers' principles and classroom practices. *Applied Linguistics, 22*(4), 470–501.

Brown, B. B. (1968). Congruity of the beliefs and practices of student teachers with Dewey's philosophy. *Educational Forum, 33*(2), 163–168.

Clark, C. M., & Peterson, P. L. (1986). Teachers' thought process. In M. C. Wittrock (Ed.), *Handbook of research in teaching* (pp. 255–296). Macmillan.

Creswell, J. W. (2012). *Qualitative inquiry and research design: Choosing among five traditions* (3rd ed.). Sage.

Creswell, J. W., Plano Clark, V. L., Gutmann, M. L., & Hanson, W. E. (2003). Advanced mixed methods research designs. In A. Tashakkori & C. Teddlie (Eds.), *Handbook on mixed methods in the behavioral and social sciences* (pp. 209–240). Sage.

Davis, M. M., & Wilson, E. K. (1999). A Title 1 teacher's beliefs, decision-making, and instruction at the third and seventh grade levels. *Reading Research and Instruction, 38*(4), 290–299.

Douglas Fir Group. (2016). A transdisciplinary framework for SLA in a multilingual world. *Modern Language Journal, 100*(S1), 19–47.

Duff, P. (2018). *Case study research in applied linguistics*. Routledge.

Fang, Z. (1996). A review of research on teacher beliefs and practices. *Educational Research, 38*(1), 47–64.

Farrell, T. S. C., & Kun, S. T. K. (2007). Language policy, language teachers' beliefs, and classroom practices. *Applied Linguistics, 29*(3), 381–403.

Farrell, T. S. C., & Lim, P. C. P. (2005). Conceptions of grammar teaching: A case study of teachers' beliefs and classroom practices. *TESL-EJ, 9*(2), 1–13.

Gao, Y. (2014). Language teacher beliefs and practices: A historical review. *Journal of English as an International Language, 9*(2), 40–56.

Gao, Y., & Bintz, W. P. (2019). An exploratory study on Chinese EFL teachers' beliefs about reading and teaching reading. *The Journal of Asia TEFL, 16*(2), 576–590.

García, O., & Li, W. (2014). Language, bilingualism and education. In O. García & L. Wei (Eds.), *Translanguaging: Language, bilingualism and education* (pp. 46–62). Palgrave Macmillan UK. https://doi.org/10.1057/9781137385765_4

Gu, P. (2017). *Exploring the context of teacher professional development: A Chinese perspective*. Foreign Language Teaching and Research Press.

Jackson, P. W. (1968). *The teacher and the machine: The Horace Mann lecture*. Pittsburgh University Press.

Johnson, K. E. (1992). The relationship between teachers' beliefs and practices during literacy instruction for non-native speakers of English. *Journal of Reading Behavior, 24*(1), 83–108.

Johnson, K. E. (1994). The emerging beliefs and instructional practices of pre-service ESL teachers. *Teaching and Teacher Education, 10*(4), 439–452.

Johnson, K. E. (2006). The sociocultural turn and its challenges for second language teacher education. *TESOL Quarterly, 40*(1), 235–257. https://doi.org/10.2307/40264518

Johnson, K. E. (2009). *Second language teacher education: A sociocultural perspective*. Routledge.

Kinzer, C. K. (1988). Instructional frameworks and instructional choices: Comparisons between preservice and in-service teachers. *Journal of Reading Behavior, 20*(4), 357–377.

Kinzer, C. K., & Carrick, D. A. (1986). Teacher beliefs as instructional influences. In J. Niles & R. Lalik (Eds.), *Solving problems in literacy: Learners, teachers & researchers* (pp. 127–134). National Reading Conference.

Konopak, B. C., Wilson, E. K., & Readence, J. E. (1994). Examining teachers' beliefs, decisions, and practices about content area reading in secondary social studies. In C. K. Kinzer & D. J. Leu (Eds.), *Multidimensional aspects of literacy research, theory, and practice: Forty-third yearbook of the National Reading Conference* (pp. 127–136). National Reading Conference.

Kuzborska, I. (2011). Links between teachers' beliefs and practices and research on reading. *Reading in a Foreign Language, 23*(1), 102–128.

Larsen-Freeman, D. (2019). Second language development in its time: Expanding our scope of inquiry. *Chinese Journal of Applied Linguistics, 42*(3), 267–284. https://doi.org/10.1515/CJAL-2019-0017

Leu, D. J., & Kinzer, C. K. (1987). *Effective reading instruction in the elementary grades.* Merrill.

Lortie, D. C. (1975). *Schoolteacher: A sociological study.* University of Chicago Press.

Martin, D. A., McMaster, N., & Carey, M. D. (2020). Course design features influencing preservice teachers' self-efficacy beliefs in their ability to support students' use of ICT. *Journal of Digital Learning in Teacher Education, 36*(4), 221–236. https://doi.org/10.1080/21532974.2020.1781000

McDonald, F., & Elias, P. (1976). *The effects of teacher performance on pupil learning: Beginning teacher evaluation study: Phase II, Final report* (Vol. 1). Educational Testing Service.

Mercer, S. (2011). Language learner self-concept: Complexity, continuity and change. *System, 39*(3), 335–346.

Morse, J. M. (1994). Designing funded qualitative research. In N. K. Denizin & Y. S. Lincoln (Eds.), *Handbook of qualitative research* (2nd ed., pp. 220–235). Sage.

Munby, J. (1982). The place of teacher beliefs in research on teacher thinking and decision making, and an alternative methodology. *Instructional Science, 11*(3), 201–225.

Ng, J., & Farrell, T. S. C. (2003). Do teachers' beliefs of grammar teaching match their classroom practices? A Singapore case study. In D. Derling, A. Q. Brown, & E. L. Low (Eds.), *English in Singapore: Research on grammar teaching* (pp. 128–137). McGraw Hill.

Richardson, V., Anders, P., Tidwell, D., & Lloyd, C. (1991). The relationship between teachers' beliefs and practices in reading comprehension instruction. *American Educational Research Journal, 28*(3), 559–586.

Shulman, L. S. (1986). Paradigms and research programs in the study of teaching. In M. C. Wittrock (Ed.), *Handbook of research on teaching* (3rd ed., pp. 1–36). Macmillan.

van der Schaaf, M. F., Stokking, K. M., & Verloop, N. (2008). Teacher beliefs and teacher behaviour in portfolio assessment. *Teaching and Teacher Education, 24*(7), 1691–1704. https://doi.org/10.1016/j.tate.2008.02.021

Wu, Y. (2005). Preface. In P. Gu (Ed.), *Exploring the context of teacher professional development: A Chinese perspective* (p. III). Foreign Language Teaching and Research Press.

Zheng, H. (2013a). The dynamic interactive relationship between Chinese secondary school EFL teachers' beliefs and practice. *The Language Learning Journal, 41*(2), 192–204. https://doi.org/10.1080/09571736.2013.790133

Zheng, H. (2013b). Teachers' beliefs and practices: A dynamic and complex relationship. *Asia-Pacific Journal of Teacher Education, 41*(3), 331–343. https://doi.org/10.1080/1359866X.2013.809051

Zheng, H. (2015). *Teacher beliefs as a complex system: English language teachers in China.* Springer International. https://doi.org/10.1007/978-3-319-23009-2

CHAPTER 2

Revisiting the Messy Construct

A Synopsis Review of Teacher Beliefs

1 From Teacher Psychology, Cognition to Beliefs

We live in an era today that is very different from the past. Fifty years ago, people were keen to explore the entities, constructs, and material items of the world; however, at present, we are increasingly interested in focusing on who we are and how we are. As teachers, we know much, if not too much, about our subject matter and content areas, but may know little about who we are and how to be good instructors. With that premise in mind, we come to understand that mastering subject matter and content area knowledge is not sufficient to be a teacher; we instead need to explore how we become and have been a teacher. Together with that premise, researchers in the educational field have been calling for the extending of teacher development, in which teacher psychology is a crucial part.

Teacher psychology is an umbrella term covering all major, interrelated concepts in the field, including (but not limited to) motivation, cognition, beliefs, attitudes, emotions, and agency. In this section, I will not elaborate on the nuances or differences among all the psychological constructs, but instead will focus on teacher beliefs. However, the construct of teacher beliefs does relate to other constructs in one way or another, so the elaboration on the term necessarily includes other exemplar constructs that proceed or follow its emergence or development.

Let's first talk about why teacher psychology matters in the current era. As teachers, we may meet with situations in which we find teaching to be a challenge. We used to or may still ascribe the cause of the challenging task to components or participants involved in the teaching journey. For example, school or institutional policies that are not in favor of implementing certain pedagogical strategies may serve as one of our reasons; students with different cultural or ethnic backgrounds that make textbook selection or activity planning difficult may serve as another; lack of resources in the underdeveloped regions may also count as one. Admittedly, all these situations may impede our teaching. However, we may always work them out under the premise that we treat ourselves as change agents and think deliberately about the solutions. Part of the reason that we are stuck in these situations is that we stop thinking, stop reflecting, and

© KONINKLIJKE BRILL NV, LEIDEN, 2022 | DOI: 10.1163/9789004506541_002

stop figuring out who we are. Therefore, our cognition and reflection count as important, if not the most important, constructs in our identities. Knowing ourselves and typically knowing how we think, believe, and behave then becomes one of the most important topics in our life-long journey as a teacher.

Teacher psychology has paved the way for teacher psychological construct studies, in which teacher cognition is one important theme. In 1968, Phillip Jackson wrote his masterpiece *Life in Classrooms* to describe and analyze teachers' mental constructs and cognitivist processes. He argued that these constructs drive teachers' behaviors. Teachers' cognition and thought processes thus began to attract researchers' attention, particularly for those working in the field of literacy education (Fang, 1996). From the mid-1970s to the early 1980s, the majority of studies were conducted on how teachers' thought processes helped teachers design and manage their classrooms and assess their students' understandings (McDonald & Elias, 1976; Shulman, 1986a). Teachers during this time viewed instruction as a means to deliver information and students as persons who decode the information. "[The] [t]eacher's responsibility basically ends when they have told students what they must remember to know and do" (Sedlak, 1987). Neither the concept of teachers' beliefs nor teachers' cognition was highly studied during this time, because educational research focused more on the teaching instead of the teachers. While the decoding way is relatively dated now, it remains popular in some developing countries, or EFL settings.

Teacher cognition studies then paved the way for the emergence of teacher belief studies (Borg, 2011). Clark and Peterson (1986) explained that the late 1970s was a time in which the dominant studies were those on teachers' cognitive lives, including studies on teacher planning, interactive thoughts and decisions, and teacher beliefs and implicit theories. It is worth mentioning that studies on teacher beliefs at that time were often by-products of studies on teacher cognition and were far less developed. Studies at this time focused on the teacher decision-making process and were concerned with how teachers plan class activities, manage classrooms, and evaluate student performance. The teacher decision-making process was thus seen as a linkage between cognition and action (Jackson, 1968); it also included multiple kinds of beliefs, each of which focused on one kind of classroom management or curriculum design dynamics (Calderhead, 1996).

In the following sections of the chapter, I will discuss the definition, nature, and features of teacher beliefs. I will also talk about the content of teacher beliefs and present reviewed findings of the existing research on the topic. I will devote a section on the evaluation of teacher beliefs. Finally, I will briefly address teacher belief studies in EFL contexts.

2   Defining Teacher Beliefs

Defining teachers' beliefs is indeed difficult. Borg (2001) stated that, "despite its [belief's] popularity, there is as yet no consensus on meaning, and the concept has acquired a rather fuzzy usage" (p. 15). Early scholars did not define teachers' beliefs in a clear way; rather, they introduced the concept of teachers' beliefs by elaborating on origins and classifications. For example, Lortie (1975) proposed that teachers' beliefs originate either from their personal experiences as students, or from their personal life experiences, such as family traditions, values, social interactions, community participation, and so forth. Clark and Peterson (1986) classified teachers' thought processes into three categories: (1) teacher planning, (2) teachers' interactive thoughts and decisions, and (3) teachers' theories and beliefs. Nespor (1987) viewed teachers' beliefs as being affective and narrative in nature and pointed out that the classroom demands the affective and evaluative method of decision-making. For example, a teacher might believe boys are better than girls in mathematics and thus assign different tasks to boys and girls in class.

Although the study of teachers' beliefs was highlighted as a key category, there had been little research about the difference between teachers' beliefs and other psychological constructs such as teachers' knowledge and attitudes in the late 1980s and the early 1990s. Therefore, Shulman (1986b) termed this period "the missing paradigm" when researchers overemphasized the knowledge of classroom practice and managerial skills by neglecting content area knowledge. Researchers thus embarked upon studies on teacher cognition, however, their emphasis was restricted only to teachers' decision-making, leaving aside the content knowledge upon which decisions are made (Meloth et al., 1989).

Pajares (1992) contributed to the topic of teacher beliefs and presented a summary that has been regarded as the most comprehensive review of the 1990s (Fang, 1996). While researchers acknowledged the importance of teachers' beliefs on the classroom decision-making process, they remained unclear about the definition for such a concept due to its large scope. Pajares further defined beliefs as "an individual's judgment that can only be inferred from a collective understanding of what human beings say, intend, and do" (1992, p. 316). Apart from defining teachers' beliefs, he also discussed what might be covered in the study of teachers' beliefs:

> [A]s with more general beliefs, educational beliefs about are required –
> beliefs about confidence to affect students' performance (teacher efficacy), about the nature of knowledge (epistemological beliefs), about

causes of teachers' or students' performance (attributions, locus of control, motivation, writing appreciation, math anxiety), about perceptions of self and feelings of self-worth (self-concept, self-esteem), about confidence to perform specific tasks (self-efficacy). There are also educational beliefs about specific subjects or disciplines (reading instruction, the nature of reading, whole language). (p. 316)

Based on Pajares' classifications above, scholars further divided teachers' beliefs into explicit and implicit ones. Espoused or explicit beliefs are what a person can readily articulate (Johnson, 1992), and implicit beliefs are held unconsciously and inferred from actions (Argyris & Schön, 1974; Breen et al., 2001). However, Borg (2011) stated that there is some disagreement on conscious vs. unconscious beliefs, with some people regarding consciousness as an inherent attribute of beliefs, and the others holding that beliefs can be either conscious or unconscious.

The concept of teachers' beliefs now refers to the evaluative or appraisal propositions that teachers hold unconsciously or consciously as true when teaching (Borg, 2001). It is often used to characterize the cognitivist structures that teachers bring when making classroom decisions (Meirink et al., 2009). Kalaja and Barcelos (2003) defined beliefs with dynamic, complex, and contradictory attributes. In other words, beliefs are socially and individually constructed, and can be shared, diversified, and uniform. This unique changing feature leads beliefs to form a complex and multilayered system (Barcelos & Kalaja, 2011; Mercer, 2011).

In the second language (L2) literature, Barcelos (2006) explained teacher beliefs from the normative, metacognitive, and contextual perspectives; beliefs were thus defined as opinions or generally inaccurate myths (normative), idiosyncratic knowledge or representations (metacognitive), or ideas interrelated with contexts and experiences of participants (contextual).

3   Nature and Features of Teacher Beliefs

It is worth mentioning that teacher beliefs differ from teacher knowledge, while the two constructs relate to each other in one way or another. Simply put, teacher knowledge is something relatively stable and objective, whereas teacher belief has a stronger affective and evaluative attribute than knowledge (Nespor, 1987). Pajares (1992) argued beliefs could be viewed as a sort of knowledge, which comes from but beyond the knowledge. For example, a teacher may hold some knowledge about a certain student, including his/her personality and classroom performance. The teacher may then believe that certain kinds of instructional or communicative strategies might be good or useful for that student. However, not all researchers agreed with the above explanation of beliefs and knowledge and instead hold the opposite opinion (Roehler et al., 1988). Many factors (including the time, epistemology, and research paradigms) may account for the emergence of the two completely different views (Ashton & Arlington, 2019; Gao, 2014). Specifically, the evolution of the research repertoire together with the ever-changing paradigms over the decades has challenged some findings in the previous research. (In the next chapter of the book, I present how research paradigms have informed the research of the teacher beliefs over the decades, typically from late 1960s to the present.)

Abelson (1979) identified seven features of a belief system that makes it different from a knowledge system:

> (1) being non-consensual; (2) denoting existential entities such as God, witches etc.; (3) acknowledging "alternative worlds"; (4) relying on evaluative and affective components; (5) including episodic material such as folklore and cultural experiences; (6) having open boundaries (including self-concept); (7) holding variable credence and having varying degrees of certitude. (as cited in Woods & Cakir, 2011, p. 383)

Abelson's classification of belief features distinguishes beliefs from knowledge in terms of the scope of truth. For beliefs, truth is individual, personal, and subjective; for knowledge, truth is objective and universal. From a theoretical, cognitivist science perspective, Abelson discussed the beliefs in general, rather than specific beliefs in reading or teaching.

Barcelos and Kalaja (2011) further studied and summarized eight characteristics of beliefs: "(1) fluctuating; (2) complex and dialectical; (3) related to the micro- and macro-political contexts and discourses; (4) intrinsically related to other affective constructs such as emotions and self-concepts; (5) other-oriented; (6) influenced by reflection and affordances; (7) related to knowledge in intricate ways"; and "(8) related to actions in complex ways" (pp. 285–286). Barcelos and Kalaja's classification embodies the tenets of sociocultural theory, which pays attention to the context in language education; it also attaches great importance to the complexity of a studied construct (Larsen-Freeman, 1997), emphasizing that the study of an emergent construct results from the study of its individual components.

Borg (2003, 2006, 2009, 2012) also presented his understanding and arguments about features of teacher beliefs, especially for those of language teachers. One of his strong arguments is the distinctive feature of core and peripheral beliefs that a teacher may hold. Borg (2012) explained in simple terms that the basic distinction between the two types of beliefs lies in their strength and stability. Core beliefs are relatively more stable and powerful in guiding our actions, whereas peripheral beliefs may be less stable and weak, leading their holders to certain compromises in action.

4 Content of Teacher Beliefs

Quite a number of articles in the existing literature, typically for those reviews on the contents of teacher beliefs (e.g., Fives et al., 2019; Zheng, 2009), drew upon Calderhead's (1996) five major types of beliefs that serve as belief content. These five major types of beliefs include: (1) teacher beliefs about learners and learning, (2) about teaching, (3) about subject matter, (4) about learning to teach, and (5) about the self and the teaching role. However, with the research scope being extended and explored, new subtypes of beliefs kept being added into the research body. For example, Hoy, Davis, and Pape (2006) argued that teacher beliefs about diversity and educational attainment should also be added to the belief system. Gao (2020b) proposed that teacher beliefs about world issues, international affairs, and transnational experiences should also be recognized in the belief system. In this section, I recluster these subsystems of beliefs and group them into three categories: beliefs about *subject matter*, *self*, and *social context*. My reclassification drew upon my learning with Jim Henderson (2007, 2015) whose 3S Understanding (*subject matter, self*, and *social*) serves originally as a theoretical framework for curriculum design but then influenced other scholars in a broader scope.

4.1 *Teacher Beliefs about Subject Matter*

Teacher beliefs about subject matter is the largest and most clear-cut category of beliefs in the belief content system. In addition to narrowly defined subject matter knowledge, which primarily comes from a teacher's specific content area, I include beliefs about curriculum, pedagogy, and education in the subject matter beliefs category. My premise is that for a teacher, these additional beliefs should be part of their overall focus and even a part of their engagement of life-long learning. This resonates with *educational beliefs* (Pajares, 1992), which is more general, broad, and encompassing. Therefore, it includes two major subsystems of beliefs: beliefs about teaching and beliefs about learning. Beliefs about teaching may further include pedagogical beliefs, curriculum beliefs, and educational beliefs, which echo beliefs about teaching and learning to teach (Calderhead, 1996). Beliefs about learning may include beliefs about learners and beliefs about general learning. I argue beliefs about learners is also a type of beliefs about learning, as we teachers keep learning about our students. Beliefs about learning may thus include beliefs about learning theories (e.g., epistemological beliefs), learning dynamics (e.g., learner motivation and agency), learner performance, etc.

4.2   Teacher Beliefs about Self

A recurring theme in this chapter is teacher beliefs as a psychological construct relate to other teacher psychological constructs and work together to help us figure out who we are and how we become or have been teachers. Teacher beliefs about *self* resonate with educational beliefs about self, self-worth, confidence, etc. (Pajares, 1992), or beliefs about the self and the teaching role (Calderhead, 1996). Recent years have witnessed a growth in the number of studies on specific self-constructs, including teacher identity and agency, which have been greatly informed by teacher experiences and beliefs (Gao, 2020b).

Teacher beliefs about self may be even more important than teacher beliefs about subject matter. Not all people agree with this and would argue that without subject matter knowledge teachers are unable to teach. I do not deny the importance of subject matter knowledge and definitely regard that knowledge to be an essential part in teaching. However, as the world has become more and more complex and materialistic, knowing and being ourselves are in a way more important than teaching what we know. We live in an era in which an increasing number of reports about teachers' misbehaviors are released every day, something that encourages us to ask ourselves how we can enhance the moral education tenets in our teaching. Therefore, our beliefs about who we are and how we are is necessary in our career trajectory.

4.3   Teacher Beliefs about Social Context

The term *social context* is aligned here with other two terms, *subject matter* and *self*, in order to echo the 3S Understanding (Henderson, 2007). However, the scope of the term *social context* here goes far beyond the traditionally or literally defined meaning of the term. I offer my operationalization of the term as any contextual environment, whether small (as in a classroom) or large (as in an international context). Teacher beliefs about social context has become increasingly important in this complex, unstable world. The expansion of international affairs, the proliferation of political policies, and the spread of transnational mobility have made intellectuals (including teachers and researchers) increasingly subject to the complexities of the world system (Gao, 2020a, 2020b). We are, to different degrees, influenced by these world dynamics.

Therefore, *teacher beliefs about social context* serves as an important belief subsystem to guide teacher decisions and behaviors, or thoughts and actions. We no longer teach in simple classrooms; we experience real-world dynamics and use our perceptions of these dynamics, either as instructional resources or as evidence, to guide our instruction. Especially when we as teachers call for social justice in education, moral learning in education, and diversity in education, we may be eager to let our students know how the sociocultural context they live in works in one way and how other contexts work in other ways. This type of beliefs about social context is thus extremely important in the current era and should be part of the holistic belief system of teachers.

5   Research on Teacher Beliefs

Studies investigating the complex relationships between teachers' beliefs and practices have been conducted over the past few decades (e.g., Borg, 2003, 2006, 2009, 2011; Farrell, 1999; Farrell & Bennis, 2013; Farrell & Lim, 2005; Johnson, 1992). The changes in the research foci are determined by the shifted paradigms; therefore, educational researchers, stretching from behaviorism to constructivism, steered from a unidirectional emphasis on the relationship between teachers' behaviors and student achievements to the correlations between teachers' cognition and beliefs and their teaching practices. Student achievements led teachers to reflect on their practices, which then enriched teachers' beliefs. In this review of the literature, I describe how studies on EFL teachers' beliefs and practices changed from an emerging stage to the current stage.

Research during the 1960s confirmed the consistent relationship between teachers' beliefs and their actual practices. Brown and Webb (1968) found that teachers' behaviors are strongly influenced by their beliefs about teaching. Brown (1962, 1963, 1966, 1968a, 1968b, 1968c) then issued a series of publications showing that "specific fundamental philosophic beliefs of teachers are even more consistently related to the observed classroom behavior of teachers than are their educational beliefs" (Brown & Webb, 1968, p. 211). Similar to Brown's findings, Harvey and his associates (Harvey 1964, 1965; Harvey et al., 1965, 1966) found that teachers' belief systems have a positive effect on teachers' behaviors. The National Institute of Education (1975) also reported that teachers' behaviors are "directed in no small measure by what they think" (p. 5).

Apart from the studies on the relationship between teachers' beliefs and practices, scholars continued to explore the origins of teachers' beliefs. Lortie (1975) stated that most teachers' teaching is almost identical to that of their prior teachers, which is termed "apprenticeship of observation":

> Teaching is unusual in that those who decide to enter it have had excep-
> tional opportunity to observe members of the occupation at work; unlike
> most occupations today, the activities of teachers are not shielded from
> youngsters. Teachers-to-be underestimate the difficulties involved, but
> this supports the contention that those planning to teach form definite
> ideas about the nature of the role. (p. 65)

Zeichner and Tabachnick (1981) further argued that the great amount of time that preservice teachers spent as pupils in the classroom shapes their beliefs, which remain latent during formal training in pedagogy at the university. Afterwards, their formed beliefs emerge as major forces when they become in-service teachers in their own classrooms.

Based on Jackson (1968), Clark and Peterson (1986) categorized teachers' thought processes into three fundamental types: (1) teacher planning, (2) teachers' interactive thoughts and decisions, and (3) teachers' theories and beliefs. Clark and Peterson's work was regarded as paramount at the time (Fang, 1996). For the first time, the topic of teachers' beliefs was formally included as a category in teacher education research. Apart from Clark and Peterson (1986), Munby (1982) also noted the lack of research on the concept of teachers' theories and beliefs. While the studies on the topic were still few, "there was nonetheless sufficient work for it to constitute a distinct category of inquiry in the field of teacher education" (Borg, 2006, p. 17).

Clark and Peterson (1986) paved the way for following scholars to explore the field of teachers' beliefs a step further. Toward defining teachers' beliefs, Pajares (1992) deconstructed the notion into a variety of foci that deserved scholars' attention for research and examination. He stated that "little will have been accomplished if research into educational beliefs fails to provide insights into the relationship between beliefs, on the one hand, and teacher practices, teacher knowledge, and student outcomes on the other" (Pajares, 1992, p. 327).

Empirical studies on language teachers' beliefs began to emerge during the 1980s and 1990s. The most significant contribution took place in the field of reading/literacy education (Fang, 1996). Harste and Burke (1977) defined reading teachers' theoretical orientations as their belief systems, which may have led teachers to monitor their students' behaviors and help them make classroom decisions. Reading research also examined how teachers' theoretical orientations affect their ways of perceiving English reading, namely, whether English reading is a bottom-up, top-down, interactive, or transactional process (Kinzer, 1988; Kinzer & Carrick, 1986; Leu & Kinzer, 1987). In addition, Mangano and Allen (1986) found that, in terms of teachers' different beliefs about writing, teachers conduct language arts instruction in different ways. Wing

(1989) stated that early childhood teachers' theoretical beliefs influence their ways of teaching, and then in turn shape their students' perceptions of reading and writing. Wing's findings are consistent with Kamil and Pearson's (1979) research, which proposed that teachers' theoretical beliefs not only affect classroom instruction, but also exert an impact on students' perceptions of literacy processes.

While it was a good starting point for studies on language teachers' beliefs, research on the topic was still flawed in some ways. For one thing, researchers narrowed the definition of teachers' beliefs, aligning them only with theoretical orientations. For another, a majority of studies presupposed that there was a unidirectional relationship between language teachers' beliefs and their practices, and what researchers did was simply test for and confirm the relationship.

6   Evaluation of Teacher Beliefs

Teacher beliefs are often analyzed and studied together with teacher cognition, and even defined as one subtype of teacher cognition (Kagan, 1990). Evaluation of teacher beliefs is thus conducted using the same or similar methodological approaches. I often compare the evaluation of psychological constructs as doing medical testing; experimenters should pay close attention to the dose of the chemicals and the use of the utensils and devices. However, it requires much effort and caution. This metaphorical statement implies the challenge of evaluating teacher beliefs and cognitions. Kagan (1990) listed four challenges that make the evaluation of teacher cognitions difficult, including: (1) the ambiguity of the notion, (2) the inability of being assessed directly, (3) the time-consuming nature of the methods, and (4) comparative judgments.

Specifically, the ambiguity of the notion refers to the idea that researchers use quite a number of these psychological construct terms interchangeably, which makes the notion hard to define and assess. The inability of being assessed directly may be explained by a couple of reasons, including the unconscious construct, which is hard to measure and describe; teachers' unwillingness to present unpopular beliefs; and contextualized beliefs which might not be generalizable to other contexts. The time-consuming nature of the methods follows the inability of being assessed directly, as indirect or comprehensive testing requires specific methods and design, resulting in longitudinal, qualitative studies. Comparative judgments refers to the different perspectives, theoretical frameworks, and paradigms that researchers use to judge and evaluate findings of the teacher belief studies.

Another contribution that Kagan (1990) made is the analyses of exemplar methods for assessing teacher beliefs. Kagan provided the reader with tables and figures to pinpoint nuances and differences among all the techniques and methods that had been used to study teacher beliefs during the 1980s. This masterpiece has been a pioneering work for the subsequent scholars who have studied teacher beliefs ever since. Kagan classified five major types of methods to evaluate teacher beliefs and each of the types includes specific techniques. The five major methods are: (1) a direct and noninferential method, which includes practical argument and Likert scale tests, (2) a method for analyzing teacher language, such as metaphors, (3) taxonomies for assessing metacognition and self-reflection, (4) a multimethod evaluation of pedagogical content knowledge/beliefs, and (5) a concept mapping method. For each method, Kagan supported the listed categories with exemplar works that had used that specific techniques or method and then provided the reader with specific critiques and comments.

Kagan (1990) further argued that each method had derived from a specific epistemological tradition. For example, psychometric test theory paved the way for Likert scale tests, cognitive mediational theory for self-reflection, and schema theory for the concept mapping method. Each method has limitations and merits which may offer insights to complement others. These epistemological traditions represent different paradigms which range from quantitative methods in positivism to qualitative methods in constructivism. (In the next chapter of the book, I elaborate on how these paradigms inform methods and techniques to study teacher beliefs.)

7   Beliefs about Languages, Reading, and EFL Teachers: An Even More
        Complex Picture

To complete this chapter and also echo to the theme of the book, I would like to focus the final section on the beliefs of language and EFL teachers. Admittedly, teachers of different types and in different content areas share common designed features across the curricula. However, they do differ in one way or another, due not only to their different subjects but also the mindsets and worldviews their different subjects bring about to them. As I will spend a whole chapter in this book talking about the features of EFL teacher beliefs, typically in the Chinese context, I will only present a summarized version of the primary features here.

The first primary feature of EFL teacher beliefs comes from its unique subject matter, the language. Many would argue that different subjects may shape people in their areas differently. However, the subject of languages is very different from subjects like mathematics in terms of shaping teacher beliefs in its dimensions. This argument connects with a broader picture in talking about how science or engineering subjects may differ from subjects in arts, humanities, and social sciences. These subjects share different fundamental philosophies, ontological and epistemological tenets, etc.; these differences in turn shape different mindsets among people and then guide them to perceive things differently. We may agree that one plus one equals two, but may diverge in how we define reading. Therefore, the unique feature of language as a subject directs beliefs of teachers in that subject matter to be different from other subjects; it makes language teacher beliefs even more *complex* than some, if not all, other subjects.

Let's take a further step in analyzing the subject of languages and focus on one of its skills, *reading*. Instead of giving a unidimensional answer to a basic math equation question, people may give different, multidimensional interpretations in defining reading, which represents different theoretical orientations (DeFord, 1979; Gao & Bintz, 2019). For example, some teachers may define reading as a way to decode messages in a given text. It represents a typical behaviorist orientation that defines reading as a decoding process. Some other teachers may then define reading as a way to process information and digest the information processed through our brain. It adds up to our repertoire and schemata. This typically represents a cognitivist orientation when reading is viewed as a cognitive mechanism in processing information. Some teachers may regard reading as a way to communicate with authors of the given text. Reading, they believe, serves as a bridge between the reader and the author. This standpoint echoes in a constructivist way when reading helps readers perceive the world and construct the meaning of the world. There are also teachers who share similar but overlapping perspectives among the above-mentioned theoretical orientations. The multiple orientations of reading make reading teacher beliefs more diverse and complex.

EFL teacher beliefs may be even more complex than language teacher beliefs in general. EFL teachers learn and teach a foreign language rather than their own mother tongue or native language. Some of the EFL teachers may even have transnational experiences, either in short-term exchange programs or long-term, degree programs, in countries where English is the native language to enhance their learning. These translanguaging and transnational experiences not only shape their identities but also change the way they perceive the world. These changed perceptions and beliefs play a crucial role in their professional settings: classrooms, schools, and institutes. They may make the teacher beliefs about self and social context different from those of teachers in other subjects.

8   Conclusion

Quite a number of review articles on teacher beliefs have been published over the years, especially in the last two decades. Some of the articles used classical literature review methods by presenting major concepts, belief contents, and methodological issues on the topic or in the field (e.g., Pajares, 1992; Fang, 1996); some recent ones used historical analysis (e.g., Gao, 2014) and meta-review methods (e.g., Fives et al., 2019). This chapter joins the review articles by revisiting these classic concepts in the literature, including the definition, the nature, and the features of teacher beliefs. It contributes an updated classification of the teacher beliefs through 3S (subject matter, self, and social). It also presented synopses on research development and evaluation of teacher beliefs over the decades. More importantly, it discussed the primary features of language and EFL teachers' beliefs that make them different from teacher beliefs in general. Some of the concepts and arguments in the chapter still require further explanation but will be elaborated on or revisited in the following chapters of the book.

References

Abelson, R. (1979). Differences between belief systems and knowledge systems. *Cognitivist Science, 3*, 355–366.

Argyris, C., & Schön, D. A. (1974). *Theory in practice: Increasing professional effectiveness.* Jossey Bass.

Ashton, J. R., & Arlington, H. (2019). My fears were irrational: Transforming conceptions of disability in teacher education through service learning. *International Journal of Whole Schooling, 15*(1), 50–81.

Ashton, P. T. (1990). Editorial. *Journal of Teacher Education, 41*(2), 2.

Barcelos, A. M. F. (2006). Researching beliefs about SLA: A critical review. In P. Kalaja & A. M. F. Barcelos (Eds.), *Beliefs about SLA: New research approaches* (pp. 7–33). Springer.

Barcelos, A. M. F., & Kalaja, P. (2011). Introduction to beliefs about SLA revisited. *System, 39*(3), 281–289.

Barnes, N., Brighton, C. M., Fives, H., & Moon, T. R. (2019). Literacy teachers' beliefs about data use at the bookends of elementary school. *The Elementary School Journal, 119*(3), 511–533. https://doi.org/10.1086/701655

Borg, M. (2001). Key concepts in ELT. Teachers' beliefs. *English Language Teaching Journal, 55*(2), 186–188.

Borg, S. (2003). Teacher cognition in language teaching: A review of research into what language teachers think, know, believe and do. *Language Teaching, 36*(2), 81–109.

Borg, S. (2006). *Teacher cognition and language education: Research and practice*. Continuum.

Borg, S. (2009). English language teachers' conceptions of research. *Applied Linguistics, 30*(3), 355–388.

Borg, S. (2011). The impact of in-service education on language teachers' beliefs. *System, 39*(3), 370–380.

Borg, S. (2012). Current approaches to language teacher cognition research: A methodological analysis. *Researching Language Teacher Cognition and Practice: International Case Studies*, 27.

Breen, M. P., Hird, B., Milton, M., Oliver, R., & Thwaite, A. (2001). Making sense of language teaching: Teachers' principles and classroom practices. *Applied Linguistics, 22*(4), 470–501.

Brown, B. B. (1962). *The relationship of experimentalism to classroom practice* [PhD dissertation]. University of Wisconsin.

Brown, B. B. (1963). Acquisition versus inquiry. *Elementary School Journal, 64*, 11–17.

Brown, B. B. (1966). Bringing philosophy into the study of teacher effectiveness. *Journal of Teacher Education, 17*(1), 35–40.

Brown, B. B. (1968a). Congruity of the beliefs and practices of student teachers with Dewey's philosophy. *Educational Forum, 33*(2), 163–168.

Brown, B. B. (1968b). *The experimental mind in education*. Harper & Row.

Brown, B. B. (1968c). *An investigation of observer-judge ratings of teacher competence: Final report, Project no. D-182*. Institute for Development of Human Resources, College of Education, University of Florida.

Brown, B. B., & Vickery, T. R. (1967). The belief gap in teacher education. *Journal of Teacher Education, 18*(4), 417–421. https://doi.org/10.1177/002248716701800408

Brown, B. B., & Webb, J. N. (1968). Research review: Beliefs and behaviors in teaching. *Association for Supervision and Curriculum Development*, 211–217.

Calderhead, J. (1996). Teachers: Beliefs and knowledge. In D. C. Berliner & R. C. Calfee (Eds.), *Handbook of educational psychology* (pp. 709–725). Prentice Hall International.

Clark, C. M., & Peterson, P. L. (1986). Teachers' thought process. In M. C. Wittrock (Ed.), *Handbook of research in teaching* (pp. 255–296). Macmillan.

DeFord, D. E. (1979). The DeFord Theoretical Orientation to Reading Profile (TORP).

DeVault, M. V., & Brown, B. B. (1967). Research. *Childhood Education, 44*(3), 205–207. https://doi.org/10.1080/00094056.1967.10729266

Fang, Z. (1996). A review of research on teacher beliefs and practices. *Educational Research, 38*(1), 47–64.

Farrell, T. S. C. (1999). The reflective assignment: Unlocking pre-service English teachers' beliefs on grammar teaching. *RELC Journal, 30*(2), 1–17.

Farrell, T. S. C., & Bennis, K. (2013). Reflecting on ESL teacher beliefs and classroom practices: A case study. *RELC Journal, 44*(2), 163–176.

Farrell, T. S. C., & Lim, P. C. P. (2005). Conceptions of grammar teaching: A case study of teachers' beliefs and classroom practices. *TESL-EJ, 9*(2), 1–13.

Fives, H., Barnes, N., Chiavola, C., SaizdeLaMora, K., Oliveros, E., & Mabrouk-Hattab, S. (2019). Reviews of teachers' beliefs. In *Oxford research encyclopedia of education.* Oxford University Press. https://doi.org/10.1093/acrefore/9780190264093.013.781

Gao, Y. (2014). Language teacher beliefs and practices: A historical review. *Journal of English as an International Language, 9*(2), 40–56.

Gao, Y. (2020a). A case study on EFL teacher beliefs and practices about reading and teaching reading. In *INTED2020 Proceedings: 14th International Technology, Education and Development Conference, Valencia, Spain, 2–4 March, 2020* (pp. 9398–9406). IATED. https://doi.org/10.21125/inted.2020

Gao, Y. (2020b). How transnational experiences and political, economic policies inform transnational intellectuals' identities and mobility: An autoethnographic study. *Higher Education Policy.* https://doi.org/10.1057/s41307-020-00187-w

Gao, Y., & Bintz, W. P. (2019). An exploratory study on Chinese EFL teachers' beliefs about reading and teaching reading. *The Journal of Asia TEFL, 16*(2), 576–590.

Harste, J. C., & Burke, C. L. (1977). A new hypothesis for reading teacher research: Both the teaching and learning of reading are theoretically based. In P. D. Pearson (Ed.), *Reading: Theory, research and practice* (pp. 32–40). National Reading Conference.

Harvey, O. J. (1964). Some cognitivist determinants of influence-ability. *Sociometry, 27,* 208–221.

Harvey, O. J. (1965). Some situational and cognitivist determinants of dissonance resolution. *Journal of Personality and Social Psychology, 1*(4), 349–355.

Harvey, O. J., & Kline, J. A. (1965). *Some situational and cognitivist determinants of role playing: A replication and extension.* Technical Report, November 15. University of Colorado.

Harvey, O. J., White, B. J., Prather, M. S., Alter, R. D., & Hoffmeister, J. K. (1966). Teachers' belief systems and preschool atmospheres. *Journal of Educational Psychology, 57*(6), 373–381.

Henderson, J. G., & Gornik, R. (2007). *Transformative curriculum leadership.* Pearson Merrill/Prentice Hall.

Hoy, A. W., Davis, H. A., & Pape, S. J. (2006). Teacher knowledge and beliefs. In P. A. Alexander & P. H. Winne (Eds.), *Handbook of educational psychology* (pp. 715–737). Lawrence Erlbaum Associates.

Jackson, P. W. (1968). *The teacher and the machine: The Horace Mann lecture.* Pittsburgh University Press.

Johnson, K. E. (1992). The relationship between teachers' beliefs and practices during literacy instruction for non-native speakers of English. *Journal of Reading Behavior, 24*(1), 83–108.

Kagan, D. M. (1990). Ways of evaluating teacher cognition: Inferences concerning the Goldilocks principle. *Review of Educational Research, 60*(3), 419–469. https://doi.org/ 10.3102/00346543060003419

Kalaja, P., & Barcelos, A. M. F. (2003). *Beliefs about SLA: New research approaches.* Kluwer Academic Publishers.

Kamil, M., & Pearson, P. D. (1979). Theory and practice in teaching reading. *New York University Education Quarterly, 10*(2), 10–16.

Kinzer, C. K. (1988). Instructional frameworks and instructional choices: Comparisons between preservice and in-service teachers. *Journal of Reading Behavior, 20*(4), 357–377.

Kinzer, C. K., & Carrick, D. A. (1986). Teacher beliefs as instructional influences. In J. Niles & R. Lalik (Eds.), *Solving problems in literacy: Learners, teachers & researchers* (pp. 127–134). National Reading Conference.

Larsen-Freeman, D. (1997). Chaos/complexity science and second language acquisition. *Applied Linguistics, 18*(2), 141–165.

Leu, D. J., & Kinzer, C. K. (1987). *Effective reading instruction in the elementary grades.* Merrill.

Lortie, D. C. (1975). *Schoolteacher: A sociological study.* University of Chicago Press.

Mangano, N., & Allen, J. (1986). Teachers' beliefs about language arts and their effects on students beliefs and instruction. In J. Niles & R. Lalik (Eds.), *Solving problems in literacy: Learners, teachers, & researchers: Thirty-fifth yearbook of the National Reading Conference* (pp. 136–142). National Reading Conference.

McDonald, F., & Elias, P. (1976). *The effects of teacher performance on pupil learning: Beginning teacher evaluation study: Phase II, Final report* (Vol. 1). Educational Testing Service.

Meirink, J. A., Meijer, P. C., Verloop, N., & Bergen, T. C. M. (2009). How do teachers learn in the workplace? An examination of teacher learning activities. *European Journal of Teacher Education, 32*(3), 209–224.

Meloth, M. S., Book, C., Putnam, J., & Sivan, E. (1989). Teachers' concepts of reading, reading instruction, and students' concepts of reading. *Journal of Teacher Education, 40*(5), 33–39.

Mercer, S. (2011). Language learner self-concept: Complexity, continuity and change. *System, 39*(3), 335–346.

Munby, J. (1982). The place of teacher beliefs in research on teacher thinking and decision making, and an alternative methodology. *Instructional Science, 11*(3), 201–225.

National Institute of Education. (1975). *Report of Panel 6, National Conference on Studies of Teaching.*

Nespor, J. (1987). The role of beliefs in the practice of teaching. *Journal of Curriculum Studies, 19*(4), 317–328.

Pajares, M. F. (1992). Teachers' beliefs and educational research: Cleaning up a messy construct. *Review of Educational Research, 62*(3), 307–332.

Roehler, L. R., Duffy, G. G., & Warren, S. (1988). Adaptive explanatory actions associated with effective teaching of reading strategies. *National Reading Conference Yearbook, 37,* 339–345.

Sedlak, M. (1987). Tomorrow's teachers: The essential arguments of the Holmes group report. *Teacher College Record, 88,* 314–326.

Shulman, L. S. (1986a). Paradigms and research programs in the study of teaching. In M. C. Wittrock (Ed.), *Handbook of research on teaching* (3rd ed., pp. 1–36). Macmillan.

Shulman, L. S. (1986b). Those who understand: Knowledge growth in teaching. *Educational Researcher, 15*(2), 4–14.

Wing, L. (1989). The influence of preschool teachers' beliefs on young children's conceptions of reading and writing. *Early Childhood Research Quarterly, 4*(1), 61–74.

Woods, D., & Cakir, H. (2011). Two dimensions of teacher knowledge: The case of communicative language teaching. *System, 39*(3), 381–390.

Zeichner, K., & Tabachnick, B. R. (1981). Are the effects of university teacher education washed out by school experiences? *Journal of Teacher Education, 32*(2), 7–11.

Zheng, H. (2009). A review of research on EFL pre-service teachers' beliefs and practices. *Journal of Cambridge Studies, 4*(1), 9.

Paradigm Shifts in Teachers' Beliefs and Practices

1 Introduction

In the previous chapter, I covered the definition, nature, and features of teacher beliefs and summarized the existing literature on teacher beliefs to present some reviewed findings. I also presented a section on the evaluation of teacher beliefs and wrapped it up by highlighting the importance of teacher belief studies in EFL contexts. If the previous chapter serves as a basket containing all the major constructs in teacher belief studies, the current chapter will be more like a sectioned briefcase, providing the reader with compartments holding similar materials that serve different functions. In other words, I will sketch a chronological, paradigm framework that presents the development of the related studies and informs the reader of how and why I came to this stage to study teacher beliefs in a pragmatic paradigm. My premise is that research paradigms are whole systems of thinking that direct established research traditions in a particular discipline (Neuman, 2011). Talking about research development is not possible without addressing its research paradigms.

Early academic research stems from positivism, in which researchers believe that no knowledge can be properly inferred or deducted unless it is evidence-based (Markie, 2004). Positivism holds that there is an objective world from which we can gather data and test it through empirical design. In the early twentieth century, some researchers began to reject positivism and embraced a qualitative research paradigm, attempting to make qualitative research as rigid as quantitative research. The 1970s and 1980s witnessed the emergence of post-positivism; the increasing ubiquity of computers aided in qualitative analysis and a number of qualitative journals came onto the stage. In the late 1980s, researchers started to study the topic of identity, including issues of race, class, and gender, which in turn resulted in a reflexive approach. However, researchers in the above paradigms were passive observers, whose theories were rejected through the 1990s, thus making qualitative research more participatory and activist-oriented. The 1990s was also a time when researchers began to develop and adopt mixed-methods approaches, having determined that a hybrid of qualitative and quantitative methods would be possible. However, while research paradigms changed as time went by, the shift was not apolitical. External factors – for example, a country's ideology – still guide what can count as publishable research in scholarship (Meyer & Benavot, 2013).

© KONINKLIJKE BRILL NV, LEIDEN, 2022 | DOI: 10.1163/9789004506541_003

The continuum of research paradigms from positivism (quantitative method-based) to pragmatism (mixed-methods-based), with other paradigms such as constructivism and transformativism (qualitative and/or quantitative method-based) in between, has reoriented EFL researchers away from simply focusing on the inconsistency/consistency of teachers' beliefs and practices toward examining the sociocultural and political factors influencing teachers' beliefs and practices. In this chapter, I provide a historical analysis of these paradigms and present how the paradigm shift has informed the development of the studies on teacher beliefs and practice.

2   Research Paradigms and Language Teacher Belief-Practice Research

While I referred to a simple definition (Neuman, 2011) at the beginning of the chapter, I find it necessary to provide other alternative definitions of the term *paradigm*. Originally, Thomas Kuhn (1962) defined the term as a way of philosophical thinking; Mackenzie and Knipe (2006) defined the term in educational research as worldviews of researchers which may represent perspectives, patterns, schools of thought, sets of shared beliefs, etc. to interpret or inform the process of data collection and analysis. Paradigms may be closely related to a researcher's beliefs and assumptions about the world (Lather, 1986) and guide the researcher's actions and investigations (Guba & Lincoln, 2005).

Four basic components that coherently interact – epistemology, ontology, methodology, and axiology – support the development of a typical paradigm (Lincoln & Guba, 1985). *Epistemology* refers to how we know the truth or reality or what counts as knowledge in the world; *ontology* looks into the nature of truth or reality; *methodology* is a researcher's logical flow of specific design procedures driven from the epistemological and ontological underpinnings; and *axiology* represents the ethical value system of the researcher (Hanson et al., 2005). Specifically, epistemology looks into the nature of knowledge rather than reality. Guiding questions used to reveal any epistemology include: What is the nature of the knowledge? What might be the relationships, if any, between the knower and the known? What might be the relationship between the researcher as the inquirer and the known? Ontology focuses on the nature of reality, existence, and being rather than knowledge. It examines the underlying beliefs of a researcher about the nature of being or reality (Scotland, 2012). As one essential construct to the paradigm, ontology helps the researcher to form their understanding of the things that constitute the world as it is known (Scott & Usher, 2004). Guiding questions used to reveal any ontology in a paradigm include: What is the nature of reality? Is reality something independent and objective, or it is something created from our minds or highly dependent on our subjective way of thinking? Methodology is the medium used to test and enhance our epistemological and ontological beliefs and carry out specific research design, data collection and analysis, and experimental procedures. The primary guiding question for a specific methodology is: How can a specific design answer the research questions and explore the constructs that help enhance the understanding of the world and reality and accrue knowledge? Axiology looks into ethnical issues that need to be considered when developing a research design or proposal. One of the simple embodiments of the term is the research consent form that researchers need to draft for, distribute to, and collect signatures from their human participants. Guiding questions for testing axiological beliefs include: What is the nature of ethics? What role do ethical values play in helping us understand the world and reality? With these general guiding questions, we (as researchers) may even ask: What ought to be done before we conduct research with our participants? Does our research do harm to any participant?

For example, a positivist paradigm presupposes that there is only one reality. Research is thus defined as an objective, unbiased way to reveal any casual relations through quantitative or statistical measurements (Lincoln & Guba, 1985). Therefore, the knower and the known are fairly independent and reality exists as an independent, objective state of being. Strict research designs that include specific (often large) sample sizes, well-planned experimental procedures, and the use of statistical software to collect and analyze the data constitute the primary methodology in a typical positivist paradigm. Ethical issues (including the potential harm to the sampled human or animal subjects or even the environment) should also be carefully considered in the positivist paradigm.

Research paradigms vary and evolve. Over recent decades paradigms have shifted from the positivist to the pragmatist. Different reviews classified the paradigms in different ways, either from different perspectives or from different disciplines. For example, Friedrich et al. (2017), working from a science or engineering perspective, reviewed paradigm shifts in information system disciplines and reported the noticeable distinction between the behavior science research paradigm and the design science research paradigm. However, this paradigm classification is in a way oversimplified and disciplined, failing to offer generalizable insights to other fields or disciplines. Hoshmand (1989), working in the area of counseling psychology (CP), offered alternate paradigms, including the natural-ethnographic, the phenomenological, the cybernetic, and other high-context paradigms, to increase the paradigm repertoire in the CP field, which had been dominated by positivist paradigms during 1980s. One of the issues in this review is that the classified paradigm terms mingled methodological terms with paradigm terms and overfocused on the methodological side.

As language teacher research falls into the general category of educational research, I refer to a classic paradigm taxonomy in the educational fields (Tashakkori & Teddlie, 2003a, 2003b), including positivism, constructivism, transformativism, and pragmatism. It is worth mentioning that terms used to title these paradigms may be varied or used interchangeably due to different times and situations. For example, *interpretivist* and *constructivist*, as well as *critical* and *transformative* are dyadic terms used interchangeably (Gao, 2014; Kivunja & Kuyini, 2017). A positivist paradigm views the world as objective being and reality and follows a strictly experimental design and scientific method of investigation to explore the world. A constructivist paradigm looks into how meaning is interpreted from a subjective way, as meanings are constructed through human experiences. A transformativist paradigm approaches the world through a critical lens and addresses social, political, and economic issues in the world. A pragmatist paradigm aims to compensate for the other paradigms by rejecting the notion that it is possible to understand the world from a single perspective. Multiple, pluralist ways, methods, and approaches are thus required to solve real-time, complex problems in the current world. The act of understanding and holding specific paradigms is meaningful to teachers and researchers as paradigms serve as the first principles to guide them in determining what to study and how to interpret the data they have collected (Denzin & Lincoln, 2000). In the sections below, I present how these classical research paradigms have informed studies on language teacher beliefs over the decades, typically in the reading or EFL fields.

2.1   *Positivism Paradigm: Debate on Consistency vs. Inconsistency*

The period from 1990 through 2000 was a time of change in the study of teachers' cognition in language education (Borg, 2003). In terms of the relationship between teachers' beliefs and teaching practices, two competing themes recurred in the relevant literature during this time. One theme proposed that a consistent relationship exists between teachers' beliefs and practices; the other, however, stated that the connection between teachers' beliefs and instruction was inconsistent.

Numerous reading studies support the notion that teachers' theoretical beliefs shape their ways of teaching. Rupley and Logan (1985) found that elementary teachers' perceptions of reading affect their decision-making in the classroom. Richardson et al. (1991) reported that teachers' beliefs about reading are consistent with their classroom teaching practices. They further explained that teachers who are in favor of skills-based instruction draw heavily on basal texts and prefer decontextualized modes of assessment, such as the ubiquitous blackline master. In contrast, teachers who believe in constructivism regard the whole-language approach as the best practice for promoting more forward-thinking teacher education programs (Anders et al., 2000; Au, 2000; Lenski et al., 1998; Pressley, 2006; Pressley & Harris, 1997). The distinction between these two opposing views of reading instruction resulted from the heavy emphasis on either behaviorism or constructivism. The latter tenet places emphasis on the *process* of learning, which has more value than the final *product*. Teachers in this constructivist paradigm serve as students' facilitators instead of instructors, allowing their curious students to stop to reflect on their learning. In contrast, teachers in the behaviorist paradigm fasten their students into seats on the bus and drive them directly to their final destination with single-minded determination.

Similar to the studies on teachers' beliefs in general and on English reading in particular, some research in ESL/EFL education focused on the relationship between language teachers' perceptions of their content knowledge and their actual teaching practices. Johnson (1992) researched certain ESL teachers' theoretical foundations in their reading classrooms and found that they aligned their actual teaching with their lesson plans. Johnson used a multidimensional TESL (teaching English as a second language) theoretical orientation profile, which consisted of an ideal instructional protocol, a lesson plan analysis task, and a beliefs inventory. She recruited as subjects 30 ESL teachers who had different theoretical orientations on second language learning and teaching, and she studied their corresponding instructional practices, represented by skill-based, rule-based, and function-based methodologies. Her findings indicated that those teachers who hold clearly defined theoretical beliefs *consistently* lean toward one particular methodological approach. In her subsequent study, Johnson (1994) concluded that while teachers' beliefs are difficult to define and study due to their invisibility, educational research on teachers' beliefs share three basic assumptions: "1) teacher beliefs influence their perceptions and judgment, 2) teacher beliefs plays a part in shaping information on teaching into classroom practices, and 3) understanding teacher beliefs may improve teacher practices and teacher education programs" (p. 439).

However, some research showed limited correspondence between teachers' beliefs and practices. Richardson et al. (1991) hypothesized that the inconsistency may be due to research methods; for example, researchers may attempt to assess teachers' beliefs through the means of paper and pencil or questionnaires. Research scholars after the 2000s further proved this hypothesis.

Basturkmen (2012) concluded that even "sophisticated methods do not necessarily reveal closer correspondence" (p. 283). In a study based on multiple sources of data on beliefs and practice, van der Schaaf et al. (2008) also
found there was no clear correspondence between teachers' stated beliefs
about research skills and their actual practices of teaching these skills in their
research classrooms. Farrell and Lim (2005) reported a "strong sense of convergence between the stated beliefs and actual classroom practices of grammar teaching of one of the two experienced teachers in their study"; however,
the beliefs of the second teacher only "partially matched some of her actual
classroom practices" (p. 9). Powers and Butler (2006) examined four teachers'
beliefs and practices in literacy and literacy assessment over the course of one
year. Four teachers worked in the university literacy clinic as part of their graduate coursework. Two of the four taught elementary pupils in a public school,
one worked as a reading resource educator at a public elementary school, and
the last one taught high school students at an alternative school affiliated with
a public school. Powers and Butler found that teachers' beliefs and their classroom instruction were often inconsistent due to an array of variables such as
school philosophy, and/or government and state mandates.

2.2   *Constructivism Paradigm: Factors Triggering the Inconsistency*
After the dominant positivism paradigm in the 1980s, researchers in the 1990s
began to explore the factors that caused these inconsistencies between teachers' beliefs and practices from a constructivist perspective. Some researchers
explained the inconsistency between teachers' beliefs and practices from a
methodological perspective, and some others held that sociocultural factors
also can account for the inconsistency.

2.2.1   Methodological Issues in Explaining the Inconsistency
Fang (1996) did a comprehensive review on teachers' beliefs and practices,
which can be regarded as a synopsis of the studies from the 1980s and 1990s.
Apart from analyzing the literature on the consistency and inconsistency
between teachers' beliefs and practices, he contributed greatly by summarizing the most commonly used methods for eliciting responses on teacher cognition. He described and analyzed three types of methods: policy capturing,
repertory grid technique, and process tracing.
    Fang (1996) defined policy capturing as a method using simulated cases or
vignettes from students, curriculum materials, or teaching episodes to study
teachers' classroom judgments. Specifically, given the features or cues in
the materials, teachers are asked to make judgments about the features. The
data are then recorded on a Likert scale and processed with linear regression

equations. The equation is interpreted as "a model of the teacher's policy about the features from which judgments are given" (p. 56). Armour-Thomas (1989) pointed out that the major problem with this method is its reliance on consistently generalizing from a small sample to a big population. Armour-Thomas also indicated other problems with the policy-capturing method. For example, a regression equation might only predict key variables that affect teachers' judgment but cannot precisely describe teachers' decision-making. Borg and Gall (1989) then listed possible errors in teacher judgments, which may include observer/experimenter drift, halo-effect, error of leniency, personal bias, reliability decay, contamination, and error of central tendency. Take the observer/experimenter drift, for example: a teacher might not understand what kinds of improvement he/she needs to make in his/her actual practice as a teacher, until he/she has the chance to observe his/her peers teaching. Other scholars also pointed out problems with the policy-capturing method (Lave, 1988; Shavelson et al., 1986). Most policy-capturing studies were conducted in laboratory settings rather than in an authentic classroom setting, which is highly dynamic and interactive. Results derived in laboratory settings may not accurately reveal the features of an authentic classroom.

Another method in which to solicit teachers' beliefs is the repertory grid technique (Johnson, 1992; Kinzer, 1988; Wilson et al., 1993). According to Fang (1996), this method is used to "discover the personal constructs that influence individual behavior." To be specific, a teacher is asked to select the statement among a set of statements which best reflects his/her teaching beliefs. Investigators label the categorical responses from teachers with "constructs," which are then put into a grid format (Clark & Peterson, 1986). Similar to the policy-capturing method, data collected from the repertory grid technique are also unreliable to be generalized to all settings. What the data represents is only hypothetical situations.

The last method used to elicit teachers' beliefs in Fang's (1996) study is process tracing. Fang regarded *process tracing* as an overarching term under which lies a group of verbal report methods used by teachers to make their classroom decisions. Four common methods are *think-aloud, retrospective interview, simulated recall,* and *journal keeping*. The think-aloud approach requires teachers to verbalize their thoughts in their actual teaching. The retrospective interview usually asks teachers to reflect upon their teaching after the class has ended, or at any moment after an instructional task has been performed. The simulated recall elicits teachers' reflection on their classroom instruction as a way of "replaying" their actual performance. The journal-keeping approach asks teachers to record their teaching practices in written form instead of verbalizing them.

Scholars hardly ever reach a consensus on the validity of the data generated from a process-tracing approach. Some hold that the introspective nature of the process-tracing method makes scholars doubt its validity in scientific research. Nisbett and Wilson (1977) criticized the use of verbalized reports as valid data and contended that self-reported data may be based on a priori and implicit casual theories. However, other scholars acknowledged the validity of a process-tracing approach and contended that:

> the inference that the recall of one's own private, conscious thoughts approximates the recall of the overt, observable events has led to the anticipation that the accuracy of the recall of conscious thought is high enough for most studies ... if the interview is made within a short time after the event. (Bloom, 1953, p. 162)

While studies on teachers' beliefs and practices in the 1980s to 1990s began to change from a one-dimensional orientation to a two-dimensional one, scholars in the 1990s still regarded the literature, at this time, as in its infancy (Bean & Zulich, 1992). Fang (1996) proposed an expanded direction for future research. First, for those scholars who believe in consistency between teachers' beliefs and practices, they should continue to explore how teachers' theoretical beliefs inform their teaching practices. Second, most studies at this time only focused on the K-12 level, with few focusing on the college level. Third, for ESL/EFL teachers, studies of the connection between teachers' beliefs and components of their content knowledge are necessary. For example, a reading teacher's beliefs can be observed through the lens of their connection with the vocabulary or grammar in a reading text. Finally, yet importantly, research should be done to gain insights from successful in-service teachers and apply them to the preservice teachers.

2.2.2   Sociocultural Factors Mediating Teachers' Beliefs and Practices
With the sociocultural theory (SCT) from Vygotsky's tenets prevailing in the contemporary academic literature, research scholars, particularly in the field of language education, began to investigate teachers' beliefs and practices through a sociocultural perspective (Johnson, 1992, 1994), which indicates that educational beliefs are not context-free (Fang, 1996; Pajares, 1992).

Therefore, there are numerous studies revealing that sociocultural factors cause the mismatch between teachers' beliefs and practices (Ajzen, 2002). Nespor (1987) explained how context plays a role in shaping teachers' beliefs and thus informing their practices: "[T]he contexts and environments within which teachers work, and many of the problems they encounter, are ill-defined and deeply entangled. ... [B]eliefs are peculiarly suited for making sense of such contexts" (p. 324). Ernest (1989) summarized two major forces that restrict teachers to align their beliefs with their actual practices: the influence from the social context and the institutionalized curriculum. All these sociocultural or contextual factors are intertwined to influence teachers' beliefs and practices. However, it is worth mentioning that studies on sociocultural factors are actually not the complete – at least not the key – embodiment of SCT theory. These factors are contextual factors which only count as part of this learning theory.

2.3 Transformativism Paradigm: Teacher Identity and Critical Pedagogy

Transformativism is among the new paradigms emerging in the new century. Transformativism, which is situated in critical theory, took teacher education in new directions. It allowed educators not only to focus on underrepresented teachers' identities but also to examine teachers' practices from the perspective of social justice and democracy.

Therefore, *positioning* emerged as a concept related to beliefs. The positioning theory sheds light on research into the interface of beliefs and identity. According to De Costa (2011, p. 350), positioning refers to how learners or teachers position themselves and others in terms of the identity they want to construct in a conversation. Positioning theory allows teachers "to examine how learners' discursive positionings shape their beliefs, and subsequently influence their learning outcomes" (p. 350). That is, how a person identifies himself or herself, together with how he or she is identified and positioned affects his/her learning outcomes. For example, Hawkins (2005) examined how two kindergarten ESL learners positioned themselves and how the way they were positioned in their learning – together with power relations indicated in the learning journey – impacted their learning outcomes.

Based on the positioning and discourse theories, Trent (2012) explored the discursive positioning of native-speaking English teachers (NET s) in Hong Kong. He studied eight NET s, using semi-structured interviews, to gain in-depth data of NET s' experiences in Hong Kong schools. He elicited responses from the eight subjects on three aspects: self-positioning (how a person identifies his/her position in a specific setting, e.g., in a conversation or a school setting), being positioned (how a person is identified by others in a specific setting), and responding to positioning (how a person responds to identities others imposed on them). Trent found that these NET s perceived challenges to their self-positioning as professional language teachers from some local teachers, who doubted the value of their teaching in the classrooms.

Another major force, critical pedagogy, which represents the transformative and advocacy paradigm, also influenced the studies on teachers' beliefs and practices to a large extent. The critical pedagogy of Freire (1970) focuses on social change and transformation of the individual. Freire seeks to liberate individuals through a dialogic problem-posing pedagogical style that challenges learners to become aware of the oppressive social structures in the world, to understand how these structures have influenced their own thinking, and to recognize their own power to change their own world.

Problem-posing processes and Freire's critical-thinking strategies have been developed across many educational situations, especially the EFL context (Merriam, 1998). Critical pedagogy changes EFL teachers' original mindset that instruction is only situated in the classroom context and instead helps teachers raise interactions with their students to a higher level, i.e., to become a community that embraces democracy and social justice. Cushner and Dowdy (2014) collected a group of teacher practitioners' classroom designs with an emphasis on social justice to the field of literacy education, among which there are many EFL researchers.

2.4   *Pragmatism Paradigm: Beliefs as a Complex System*

Pragmatism (Dewey, 1929; James, 1907; Peirce, 1995) is an action-oriented philosophy of science that reveals the link between action and truth, or practice and theory. Dewey (1933) defines pragmatism as "the doctrine that reality possesses practical character" (p. 31). Pragmatism focuses on the real-world problems that are too complicated to solve from just a single paradigm. Pragmatism does not require researchers to generate a universal solution to a single problem, but instead leads them to identify and analyze the actual situations in which all factors are interconnected to make the complex picture. The pragmatism paradigm is also indicated in the studies on EFL teachers' beliefs and practices when researchers attempt to identify teachers' beliefs as a complex system.

In terms of the research methods and approaches, pragmatism attempts to address the gap between the structuralist, scientific methods and the naturalist, interpretive methods. In other words, quantitative methods and qualitative methods work together to provide support to the pragmatism paradigm (Creswell, 2012; Creswell & Clark, 2007). It is worth mentioning that the pragmatism paradigm does not weigh any particular approach over others, nor give priority to any research orientation. Instead, the paradigm is concerned about how real-world problems can be solved through a combination of methods and approaches. However, it does take steps and procedures to implement a certain design in the pragmatism paradigm, because pragmatists believe that the process of acquiring knowledge is a continuum. Positivism typically supports quantitative methods to generate deductive reasoning and constructivism particularly adopts qualitative approaches for inductive reasoning.

Pragmatism, however, embraces the two extremes and adjusts approaches in the continuum (Feilzer, 2010).

While few studies have been conducted to align complex dynamic systems theory strictly with the pragmatic paradigm, hints or clues from the existing literature can still be found to support this argument. Van Geert (2011) argued that CDS is "pragmatic" in nature (p. 277) and expected a paradigm shift from the dominant paradigm that is too empirical in developmental psychology to be an evolutionary, pragmatic one. He was pessimistic about this kind of paradigm shift, as he argued that developmental psychology is deeply rooted in empirical studies that positivism serves as the dominant paradigm. Having said that, he still advocated for "a velvet evolution of developmental psychology" (p. 277).

Pragmatism as a research paradigm caters to scholars' needs to deal with issues in the ever-changing world. This is particularly true for studies on teacher beliefs. Barcelos and Kalaja (2011) stated that "[t]he studies tend to view beliefs as variable and fixed, and focus on changes on these, and/or on the interaction between beliefs and learner or teacher actions, acknowledging their relationship to be a complex one" (p. 281). Therefore, studies on language teachers' beliefs in the recent two decades tend to focus on the two following aspects: beliefs as a complex system and how beliefs interact with actions.

How beliefs interact with actions has been a recurring theme in scholarly research for decades. Earlier research on beliefs viewed this relationship as a unidirectional, cause-and-effect one; as interactive and mutual, namely, beliefs influence actions and vice versa; or, as complex, that is, beliefs and practices may be irrelevant due to contextual factors (Barcelos, 2006). Rather than studying the effects of teachers' beliefs on practices, researchers in the new era began to investigate the role of actions in beliefs change from sociocultural and ecological perspectives. Most research through the lens of a sociocultural approach regarded beliefs as mediators of learner/teacher actions (Navarro & Thornton, 2011), and reflection on their actions helps them define their emergent beliefs. Generally, research on language teachers' beliefs and practices in a sociocultural approach can be categorized as follows: (a) belief as a mediator and (b) belief change.

2.4.1   Belief as a Mediator

Alanen (2003) argued that "further research is needed to investigate how beliefs are put to practice during language learning" (p. 68). To bridge the gap, Negueruela-Azarola (2011) investigated how "semiogenesis" – an approach referring to "documenting the emergence of meaning as signs with functional capabilities in concrete activity" – informs the internalization of beliefs as conceptualizing activity, "the origin and result of developmental processes in the L2 classroom" (p. 363). Eight in-service language teachers were recruited in the study and given a seminar on sociocultural approaches in L2 teaching. A series of text-books, articles, and book chapters on L2 teaching were selected and assigned to the participants to elicit their discussion and reflection. In the study, Negueruela-Azarola viewed a sociocultural framework as a "complementary path to exploring beliefs as contextually situated social meaning emerging in specific sense-making activities" (p. 368).

Similar to Negueruela-Azarola, other scholars have used the sociocultural framework to investigate beliefs (see Barcelos & Kalaja, 2011; Yang & Kim, 2011; Peng, 2011; De Costa, 2011). These papers report on how beliefs act as mediators in cognition, in change, and in the macro-political context (Barcelos & Kalaja, 2011).

2.4.2   Belief Change

There are also some recent studies focusing on belief change (Borg, 2011; Navarro & Thornton, 2011; Aragão, 2011; Mercer, 2011; Borg, 2011; Woods & Cakir, 2011). Mercer (2011) noted that beliefs are complex and nuanced and may alter to "reflect contextual changes."

Reflection plays an important role in belief change. Woods and Cakir (2011) stated that, "when a teacher reflects on practice, and begins to articulate his or her 'practical' knowledge, it begins to be theorized and to inform his or her theoretical knowledge" (p. 389). By acknowledging the changeable attributes of teacher beliefs, Woods and Cakir (2011) argued that the teachers' knowledge and beliefs in communicative language teaching is "multidimensional" and "dynamic." They developed a framework with two dimensions: "personal-impersonal" and "theoretical-practical" (p. 381). Then, they investigated six Turkish English teachers and found that when those teachers discussed the characteristics of communicative teaching, depending on their own experiences and stories, they referred to theoretical frameworks learned at school. It turns out that they relied on their personal/practical beliefs more than impersonal/theoretical beliefs.

Borg (2011) investigated how teacher education courses affect in-service teachers' beliefs and concluded that these education courses do have an impact. These education courses can extend teachers' beliefs and make their beliefs more explicit. They also help teachers to articulate their beliefs and put them into practice, thus connecting their beliefs with theory, and they can ultimately pave the way for teachers to form new beliefs. Borg also suggested in his study that educational courses "could have engaged teachers in a more productive and sustained examination of their beliefs" (2011, p. 370).

Besides the studies on teachers' beliefs from a sociocultural perspective, research regarding how teachers perceive reading shapes their ways of teaching reading remains prevalent after the 2000s (Arnett & Turnbull, 2008; Borg, 2011; Isikoglu et al., 2009). Other scholars (Sato & Kleinsasser, 2004; Breen et al., 2001) even found that the relationship between language teachers' beliefs and practices is interactive, namely that, "beliefs drive actions, but experiences and reflection on actions can lead to changes in, or additions, to beliefs themselves" (Basturkmen, 2012, p. 283).

Fung and Chow (2002) indicated that there was limited correspondence between the novice teachers' theoretical orientations and their practices during a language teaching practicum. Basturkmen and others (2004) investigated the relationship between foreign language teachers' beliefs and practices in terms of "focus on form," which are the instances of the behaviorist orientation during communicative lessons. They concluded that, among the three teachers, there was a "tenuous relationship" (p. 243) between the teachers' actual practices and stated beliefs.

3   The Influx of Paradigms in the New Era

The shifts of the paradigms entail the development and advances of the research. The above review so far has offered a synopsis on how research paradigms inform the changes and development of studies on language teacher beliefs and practices. However, as paradigms move and shift, they also provide us with challenges to figure out the paradigm that best fits a particular study. In addition, the constant changes that the world brings about cause us to believe there might not exist a one-size-fits-all paradigm. Therefore, the influx of paradigms has guided the development of research in the new era.

To give the reader a better picture, I offer the table below (see Table 2), presenting how the evolution of research paradigms directs the evolution of ontology, theoretical orientations, methodological approaches, and constructs studied. In particular, I provide the reader with exemplar studies for a specific paradigm.

While I have offered my explanation of the table, I still intend to provide the reader with more statements regarding the limitation of the table: First, shifts of these paradigms does not entail any replacement of one paradigm over the precedent one. Scientific research now has gone to a stage where pluralism dominates the arena, indicating multiple paradigms coexist in the current research academia. Boundaries of these paradigms while being constantly

TABLE 2   Overview of language teacher belief-practice studies

Paradigms	Ontology	Epistemology	Theoretical orientations	Methodological approach	Constructs studied	Reading models	Exemplar studies
Positivism	Empirical, individualist	Linguistic reality; Reified mental constructs; mind as a container	Behaviorist; Cognitivist	Experimental design; Surveys; Think-aloud protocols; Classroom observations; Document analysis	Consistency between beliefs & practices	Bottom-up; decoding; skill-based; Top-down; meaning-based whole language approach	Johnson (1992, 1994); Golombek (1998); Borg (2001); Breen et al., (2001)
Constructivism	Social, contextual	Participation metaphor	Interactionist; Holistic	Discourse analysis; Case studies; Interviews; Narratives; Group discussion	Factors or influences informing the interaction btw beliefs & practices	Interactive	Borg (2011); Li (2013); Moodie & Feryok (2015); Crookes (2015); Coffey (2015); Farrell & Lim (2005); Farrell & Bennis (2013)
Transformativism	Sociohistorical; Critical & ethical	Knowing in action; student learning; Through shared intentions	Sociocultural; Critical theory	Ethnography; Grounded theory; Focus group interviews	Teacher belief & identity, agency, intentionality, etc.	Transactional	Feryok (2010); Golombek (2015); Johnson (2015)
Pragmatism	Complex, dynamic, chaotic, systemic, nonlinear, pluralist, etc.	Emergent sense making; Multiple realities	Ecological; CDST	Exploratory sequential mixed-methods; Explanatory sequential mixed-methods	Belief changes; Evolutionary interaction btw beliefs & practices	An influx of models: - New literacy - Multimodal - Extensive reading, etc.	Svalberg (2015); Feryok & Oranje (2015); Zheng (2015)

claimed over the years are still to some extent overlapping, as these boundaries indicate the transition from one paradigm to another.

In addition, analysis and categorization of the related studies is admittedly subjective, while I attempted to provide critical, rigorous analyses on these articles. This might be the room for open debate, as even the authors of these articles may find it sometimes difficult to categorize their works strictly into certain domain.

Also, I only provide some exemplar, empirical studies on language teacher beliefs and practices. The conceptual studies are not in the scope of the table, as methodological approaches are hardly fit for these conceptual pieces. However, I do not deny the contributions or merits of these conceptual studies. Besides, I do not assign superiority but only give credit to the selected examples, as I believe that many other empirical studies while not being selected for the current table are academically excellent.

I referred to Burns, Freeman, and Edwards (2015) when drawing this paradigm and literature table. However, several adaptations were made according to nuances between my understanding and theirs. These nuances may indicate certain *thought divergences* (I don't term them as *disagreements*, as I believe they are about perspectives). One of the nuances is about the belonging of the ecological view they assigned in their conceptual piece (Burns et al., 2015). They tentatively assigned social ontology as the place to which the ecological view as a theoretical framework may belong. However, I believe the view more suitable for the complex, chaotic system. Many scholars reported the similarities of the ecological view and the CDST perspective (e.g., Feryok, 2010; Feryok & Oranje, 2015), arguing that changes and emerging states from a CDST perspective may resemble those in an ecological system. I understand how Burns, Freeman, and Edwards (2015) paired holistic and ecological views together in their pieces and put them under the theoretical framework on the social track, because changes in teachers' practices are identified as "ecologies of practices" (p. 596); however, I argue that changes in teachers' practices catering to the changes in their minds and beliefs may indicate efforts teachers had made to align practices and beliefs in an interactive way. The interactionist rather than the ecological view may better present the theoretical foundations in the social ontology. However, it may be seen as a start for the ecological perspective, while it hardly went deeper about the changes or evolving states of elements studied. In addition, the two terms still differ from each other at their core: the holistic perspective, while also presenting a tendency to include all the elements of a system, fails to depict the evolving, evolutionary, and changing states of these elements; the ecological perspective, however, emphasizes these evolving, evolutionary, and changing states, which echo the tenets in a typical CDST perspective.

Some of the exemplar studies in the table were introduced in the historical analysis part of the chapter. I thus won't repeat elaborating these studies in the following part; instead, I will be focusing on exemplar studies in the recent six years, starting from 2015 to 2021. I will start with some synoptic analyses on language teacher cognition studies published in a special issue of *The Modern Language Journal* in 2015. This issue presented eight articles addressing the development of language teacher cognition studies through paradigm shifts; the individualist ontology (the positivist camp) was no longer adopted among the eight articles. Instead, the eight articles primarily fell into social, sociohistorical, and complex ontologies. Four of the articles (Coffey, Crookes, Kubanyiova, and Moodie & Feryok) adopted social ontological perspectives on language teacher and varied their constructs studied and the methodological approaches used. It is worth mentioning that while the eight articles all focused on language teacher cognition, strictly speaking, only Feryok and Oranje (2015) was concerned with language teacher beliefs. Specifically, the article examined how a German foreign language teacher believed cultural portfolio projects to be effective in informing practical challenges in intercultural communicative language teaching. Through a qualitative interview and a microgenetic analysis of a classroom session, the authors found some evidence confirming the convergence of a teacher's beliefs and practices. Feryok and Oranje (2015) used the dynamic system theory as their theoretical lens, which is in accordance to Feryok's other studies (e.g., Feryok, 2010).

While the special issue fails to identify a positivist paradigm and an individualist ontology in the collection, studies in the new era still witness an influx of paradigms and constructs studied. For example, in a conceptual piece Phakiti and Plonsky (2018) discussed how ten beliefs could be reconciled with linguistic theories and approaches in SLA. The idea of reconciling beliefs with theories and approaches remains a way to connect to the positivist paradigm. Likewise, a couple of studies are still in the cognitive paradigm, exploring psychological factors, including language awareness (e.g., van den Broek et al., 2018), language prejudice (e.g., Metz, 2019), or pro-multilingual beliefs (e.g., Bernstein et al., 2021). Constructs that scholars focus on and choose to study for the language teacher beliefs and practices are much more diverse and complex, compared with the studies from before 2015. For example, instead of focusing on single, specific language skills (including reading and writing), an increasing number of studies are focused on multilingual pedagogies (e.g., Portoles & Marti, 2020), language ideologies (e.g., Alisaari et al., 2019; Metz, 2019), information and communication technology (e.g., Chen et al., 2021; Liu et al., 2017), and, in particular, corrective feedback (e.g., Bao, 2019; Kartchava et al., 2020).

One of the contributions that I attempted to make to the chart in Table 2 is an addition of the reading models. It is worth mentioning that the reading models are not aligned to the specific, exemplar studies listed there, but instead are simply representatives of the research paradigms, epistemologies, ontologies, and theoretical orientations. In addition, while scholars (e.g., Kubanyiova & Feryok, 2015) attempted to reclaim the boundaries of paradigms and exemplar studies, it is unrealistic to draw crystal-clear boundaries: the development of scientific research includes many transitions among different paradigms and epistemologies; these transitions entail the blurring of the boundaries. Therefore, the classification of these reading models and the alignment of the models with the paradigms may to some extent be subjective, but not arbitrary.

Generally, four types of reading models may cater to four paradigms, and each type may include more than one single reading model. Specifically, the bottom-up model influenced by reading theorists including Gough (1972) and LaBerge and Samuels (1974) who defined reading from a language decoding perspective and believed that English reading means literally the mechanical process of going through materials or text printed or written in the English language (Zainal, 2003). The top-down model is different from the bottom-up model, which focuses on text, words, and materials. A top-down model by Ken Goodman (1967) and Smith (1971) focuses on the comprehension and information processing of the text, words, or materials. It is a model based on higher order mental processes instead of the physical text on the page. Therefore, meaning takes precedence over structure. Regardless of the bottom-up or the top-down model, they both regard reading as a linear process, which represents a typical positivist, behaviorist idea.

An interactive reading model (Rumelhart, 1977) combines both bottom-up and top-down models. Typical beliefs in this model argue that good readers are both good decoders and good interpreters of the text. Therefore, the model strives to develop readers' skills and strategies in a meaningful context. Behind the model stands a constructivist, interactionist idea and views reading as a holistic process.

Leading is the model by Rosenblatt (1986), a transactional reading model that holds that both the reader and the text play important roles in the meaning-formation process. In other words, meaning is formed by continuous transaction between the reader and the text. Through the many transactions, deep meaning or language awareness emerge. Therefore, a transformativist paradigm may represent the underpinning philosophy behind the transactional model.

The last type of reading model is a pragmatic reading model. Different from other specific reading models, the reading model behind a pragmatist paradigm is actually an influx of reading models. It may include the new literary model, which explores how technology has informed reading in the current era; the multimodal model, which focuses on the modes, modalities, semiotics, and symbols involved in the reading process; and/or the extensive reading model, which derives from Renandya (2007).

As the aim of the book is to explore reading teachers' beliefs and practices, it is necessary to make the above statements debriefing how reading models are connected with research paradigms, shifts of epistemologies and ontologies, as well as theoretical orientations. (Further elaboration of these reading models and research paradigms will be presented in the chapters to follow.)

4   Theoretical Paradigm Selected for the Present Study

While the topic of teachers' beliefs has been studied for decades, there is still more room for exploration in this field. First, studies on language teachers' beliefs and their practices in teaching specific language knowledge are unevenly distributed. For example, as reported above, a great number of the studies focus on grammar teaching (Andrews, 1997, 1999; Basturkmen et al., 2004; Borg, 1999a, 1999b, 2001; Burgess & Etherington, 2002; Farrell, 1999; Farrell & Lim, 2005). There are surprisingly fewer studies on language teachers' beliefs and practices than on other specific aspects of language teaching, such as speaking, listening, writing, vocabulary, and even comprehension. Even within the larger portion of studies on grammar and reading, the correlation between teachers' beliefs and their classroom actions still needs to be investigated further due to newly emergent and interdisciplinary theories.

Second, with an increasing number of paradigms emerging to influence the studies on teachers' beliefs and practices, researchers should address the topic from multiple, instead of single, paradigms. This is especially true since the Douglas Fir Group (2016) paved the way for a *transdisciplinary framework* and García and Li (2014) shed light on the *multilingual turn* in the middle of the 2010s. Using multiple methods can better refine the design than a single method. For example, instead of a belief inventory and case studies, more reflection and interpretative approaches can be used to examine the issues in the field of teachers' beliefs and practices.

Therefore, the present study was conducted through the lens of pragmatism, which is not committed to any specific philosophy or reality, but instead to the complexity of real-world problems (Cherryholmes, 1992; Murphy, 1990). Scholars and researchers using the pragmatism paradigm acknowledge the existence of divergences, inconsistencies, and barriers in social, historical, political, and other contexts. Over recent decades, scholars in this paradigm have used a mixed-methods approach to collect both quantitative and qualitative data that best answer their research questions. LeCompte and Schensul (1999) used both quantitative and qualitative data collection in their ethnographic study; current researchers (e.g., Luck et al., 2006; Yin, 2003) frequently use both quantitative and qualitative data in their case studies. Therefore, the present study, designed in a mixed-methods approach, best fits the pragmatism paradigm by combining the quantitative approach and the qualitative approach. First, the quantitative approach is used to test the (in)consistency or the interaction between the Chinese EFL teachers' beliefs and practices. Then, the qualitative approach is adopted to inform the results from the quantitative design. Surveys, classroom observations, and interviews are sequentially used for data collection and analysis in the study. The specific theoretical framework used for the study is the complex dynamic systems theory, which will be explained in Chapter 4.

5 Conclusion

One of the core components in the book is belief. For researchers, their guiding beliefs derive from their research paradigms. Therefore, in this chapter, I presented a historical analysis on the evolution of research paradigms, typically tailored to the studies on teacher beliefs and practices. The paradigm shift directs research on the topic from a monolingual, positivist view to a pragmatist, multilingual one, and thus yielded studies with diversified, multifaceted findings. Through the historical analysis, I ended the chapter with my rationale for why pragmatism works best as the research paradigm for my study or studies like mine. My analysis and interpretation of the pragmatist research paradigm paved the way for the theoretical framework selected for the study, which will be presented in the next chapter.

Acknowledgment

Part of the chapter has been published as Gao, Y. (2014). Language teacher beliefs and practices: A historical review. *Journal of English as an International Language, 9*(2), 40–56. While adaptation has been thoroughly made for the current chapter, credits are still acknowledged for my publication and the journal.

References

Ajzen, I. (2002). Perceived behavioral control, self-efficacy, locus of control, and the theory of planned behavior. *Journal of Applied Social Psychology, 32*(4), 1–20.

Alanen, R. (2003). A sociocultural approach to young learners' beliefs about language learning. In P. Kalaja & A. M. F. Barcelos (Eds.), *Beliefs about SLA: New research approaches* (pp. 55–85). Kluwer Academic Press.

Alisaari, J., Heikkola, L. M., Commins, N., & Acquah, E. O. (2019). Monolingual ideologies confronting multilingual realities: Finnish teachers' beliefs about linguistic diversity. *Teaching and Teacher Education, 80,* 48–58. https://doi.org/10.1016/j.tate.2019.01.003

Anders, P. L., Hoffman, J. V., & Duffy, G. G. (2000). Teaching teachers to teach reading: Paradigm shifts, persistent problems, and challenges. In M. L. Kamil, P. B. Mosenthal, P. D. Pearson, & R. Barr (Eds.), *Handbook of reading research* (Vol. 3, pp. 719–742). Erlbaum.

Andrews, S. (1997). Metalinguistic knowledge and teacher explanation. *Language Awareness, 6*(2/3), 147–161.

Andrews, S. (1999). All these like little name things: A comparative study of language teachers' explicit knowledge of grammar and grammatical terminology. *Language Awareness, 8*(3/4), 143–159.

Aragao, R. (2011). Beliefs and emotions in foreign language learning. *System, 39*(3), 302–313.

Armour-Thomas, E. (1989). The application of teacher cognition in the classroom: A new teaching competency. *Journal of Research and Development in Education, 22*(3), 29–37.

Arnett, K., & Turnbull, M. (2008). Teacher beliefs in second and foreign language teaching: A state-of-the-art review. In H. J. Sisken (Ed.), *From thought to action: Exploring beliefs and outcomes in the foreign language program* (pp. 9–29). Thomson Heinle.

Au, K. (2000). A multicultural perspective on policies for improving literacy achievement: Equity and excellence. In M. L. Kamil, P. B. Mosenthal, P. D. Pearson, & R. Barr (Eds.), *Handbook of reading research* (Vol. 3, pp. 835–851). Lawrence Erlbaum Associates.

Bao, R. (2019). Oral corrective feedback in L2 Chinese classes: Teachers' beliefs versus their practices. *System, 82,* 140–150. https://doi.org/10.1016/j.system.2019.04.004

Barcelos, A. M. F. (2006). Researching beliefs about SLA: A critical review. In P. Kalaja & A. M. F. Barcelos (Eds.), *Beliefs about SLA: New research approaches* (pp. 7–33). Springer.

Barcelos, A. M. F., & Kalaja, P. (2011). Introduction to beliefs about SLA revisited. *System, 39*(3), 281–289.

Basturkmen, H. (2012). Review of research into the correspondence between language teachers' stated beliefs and practices. *System, 40*(2), 282–295. https://doi.org/10.1016/j.system.2012.05.001

Basturkmen, H., Loewen, S., & Ellis, R. (2004). Teachers' stated beliefs about incidental focus on form and their classroom practices. *Applied Linguistics, 25*(2), 243–272.

Bean, T. W., & Zulich, J. (1992). A case study of three preservice teachers' beliefs about content area reading through the window of student-professor dialogue journals. In C. Kinzer & D. J. Leu (Eds.), *Literacy research, theory, and practice: Views from many perspectives* (pp. 463–474). NRC.

Bernstein, K. A., Kilinc, S., Troxel Deeg, M., Marley, S. C., Farrand, K. M., & Kelley, M. F. (2021). Language ideologies of Arizona preschool teachers implementing dual language teaching for the first time: Pro-multilingual beliefs, practical concerns. *International Journal of Bilingual Education and Bilingualism, 24*(4), 457–480. https://doi.org/10.1080/13670050.2018.1476456

Bloom, B. S. (1953). Thought processes in lectures and discussions. *Journal of General Education, 7,* 160–170.

Borg, M. (2001). Key concepts in ELT. Teachers' beliefs. *English Language Teaching Journal, 55*(2), 186–188.

Borg, S. (1998). Teachers' pedagogical systems and grammar teaching: A qualitative study. *TESOL Quarterly, 32*(1), 9–38. https://doi.org/10.2307/3587900

Borg, S. (1999a). Studying teacher cognition in second language grammar teaching. *System, 27*(1), 19–31. https://doi.org/10.1016/S0346-251X(98)00047-5

Borg, S. (1999b). The use of grammatical terminology in the second language classroom: A quality study of teachers' practices and cognitions. *Applied Linguistics, 20*(1), 95–124. https://doi.org/10.1093/applin/20.1.95

Borg, S. (2003). Teacher cognition in language teaching: A review of research into what language teachers think, know, believe and do. *Language Teaching, 36*(2), 81–109.

Borg, S. (2011). The impact of in-service education on language teachers' beliefs. *System, 39*(3), 370–380.

Borg, W. R., & Gall, M. D. (1989). *Educational research: An introduction* (5th ed.). Longman.

Breen, M. P., Hird, B., Milton, M., Oliver, R., & Thwaite, A. (2001). Making sense of language teaching: Teachers' principles and classroom practices. *Applied Linguistics, 22*(4), 470–501.

Burgess, J., & Etherington, S. (2002). Focus on grammatical form: Explicit or implicit? *System, 30*(4), 433–458.

Burns, A., Freeman, D., & Edwards, E. (2015). Theorizing and studying the language-teaching mind: Mapping research on language teacher cognition. *The Modern Language Journal, 99*(3), 585–601. https://doi.org/10.1111/modl.12245

Chen, X., Shu, D., & Zhu, Y. (2021). Investigating in-service foreign language teachers' beliefs about using information and communication technology. *Asia-Pacific Education Researcher, 30*(1), 59–70. https://doi.org/10.1007/s40299-020-00514-0

Cherryholmes, C. (1992). Notes on pragmatism and scientific realism. *Educational Researcher, 21*(6), 13–17.

Clark, C. M., & Peterson, P. L. (1986). Teachers' thought process. In M. C. Wittrock (Ed.), *Handbook of research in teaching* (pp. 255–296). Macmillan.

Creswell, J. W. (2012). *Qualitative inquiry and research design: Choosing among five traditions* (3rd ed.). Sage.

Creswell, J. W., & Plano Clark, V. L. (2007). *Designing and conducting mixed methods research*. Sage.

Crookes, G. (2015). Redrawing the boundaries on theory, research, and practice concerning language teachers' philosophies and language teacher cognition: Toward a critical perspective. *Modern Language Journal, 99*(3), 485–499.

Cushner, K., & Dowdy, J. (Eds.). (2014). *From the margins to the mainstream: Enhancing social awareness in the social studies classroom*. Rowman & Littlefield.

De Costa, P. I. (2011). Using language ideology and positioning to broaden the SLA learner beliefs landscape: The case of an ESL learner from China. *System, 39*(3), 347–358.

Denzin, N. K., & Lincoln, Y. S. (Eds.) (2000). *Handbook of qualitative research*. Sage.

Dewey, J. (1929). *The quest for certainty: A study of the relation of knowledge and action*. Minton, Balch and Co.

Dewey, J. (1933). *How we think: A restatement of the relation of reflective thinking to the educative process*. D. C. Heath & Co.

Douglas Fir Group. (2016). A transdisciplinary framework for SLA in a multilingual world. *Modern Language Journal, 100*(S1), 19–47.

Ernest, P. (1989). The impact of beliefs on the teaching of mathematics. In P. Ernest (Ed.), *Mathematics teaching: The state of the art* (pp. 249–254). Falmer Press. http://socialsciences.exeter.ac.uk/education/research/centres/stem/publications/pmej/impact.htm

Fang, Z. (1996). A review of research on teacher beliefs and practices. *Educational Research, 38*(1), 47–64.

Farrell, T. S. C. (1999). The reflective assignment: Unlocking pre-service English teachers' beliefs on grammar teaching. *RELC Journal, 30*(2), 1–17.

Farrell, T. S. C., & Bennis, K. (2013). Reflecting on ESL Teacher Beliefs and Classroom Practices: A Case Study. *RELC Journal, 44*(2), 163–176. https://doi.org/10.1177/0033688213488463

Farrell, T. S. C., & Lim, P. C. P. (2005). Conceptions of grammar teaching: A case study of teachers' beliefs and classroom practices. *TESL-EJ, 9*(2), 1–13.

Feilzer, M. Y. (2010). Doing mixed methods research pragmatically: Implications for the rediscovery of pragmatism as a research paradigm. *Journal of Mixed Methods Research, 4*(1), 6–16.

Feryok, A. (2010). Language teacher cognitions: Complex dynamic systems? *System, 38*(2), 272–279. https://doi.org/10.1016/j.system.2010.02.001

Feryok, A., & Oranje, J. (2015). Adopting a cultural portfolio project in teaching German as a foreign language: Language teacher cognition as a dynamic system. *Modern Language Journal, 99*(3), 546–564.

Freire, P. (1970). *Education for critical consciousness.* Seabury.

Friedrich, T., Schlauderer, S., Weidinger, J., & Raab, M. (2017). On the research paradigms and research methods employed in the bise journal – A ten-year update. In J. M. Leimeister & W. Brenner (Eds.), *Proceedings der 13. Internationalen Tagung Wirtschaftsinformatik (WI 2017)* (pp. 1111–1125).

Fung, L., & Chow, L. P. Y. (2002). Congruence of student teachers' pedagogical images and actual classroom practices. *Educational Research, 44*(3), 313–322.

Gao, Y. (2014). Language teacher beliefs and practices: A historical review. *Journal of English as an International Language, 9*(2), 40–56.

García, O., & Li, W. (2014). Language, bilingualism and education. In O. García & L. Wei (Eds.), *Translanguaging: Language, bilingualism and education* (pp. 46–62). Palgrave Macmillan UK. https://doi.org/10.1057/9781137385765_4

Golombek, P. R. (1998). A study of language teachers' personal practical knowledge. *TESOL Quarterly, 32*(3), 447–464.

Goodman, K. S. (1967). Reading: A psycholinguistic guessing game. *Journal of the Reading Specialist, 6,* 126–135.

Gough, P. B. (1972). One second of reading. In J. F. Kavanagh, & I. G. Mattingly (Eds.), *Language by ear and by eye* (pp. 331–358). MIT Press.

Guba, E. G., & Lincoln, Y. S. (1994). Competing paradigms in qualitative research. In N. K. Denzin & Y. S. Lincoln (Eds.), *Handbook of qualitative research* (pp. 105–117). Sage.

Guba, E. G., & Lincoln, Y. S. (2005). Paradigmatic controversies, contradictions, and emerging confluences. In N. K. Denizin & Y. S. Lincoln (Eds.), *Handbook of qualitative research* (3rd ed., pp. 191–215). Sage.

Hanson, W. E., Creswell, J. W., Clark, V. L. P., Petska, K. S., & Creswell, J. D. (2005). Mixed methods research designs in counseling psychology. *Journal of Counseling Psychology, 52,* 224–235.

Hawkins, M. (2005). Becoming a student: Identity work and academic literacies in early schooling. *TESOL Quarterly, 39*(1), 59–85.

Hoshmand, L. L. S. T. (1989). Alternate research paradigms: A review and teaching proposal. *The Counseling Psychologist, 17*(1), 3–79. https://doi.org/10.1177/0011000089171001

Isikoglu, N., Basturk, R., & Karaca, F. (2009). Assessing in-service teachers' instructional beliefs about student-centered education: A Turkish perspective. *Teaching and Teacher Education, 25*(2), 350–356.

James, W. (1907). *Pragmatism: A new way for some old ways of thinking.* Longmans, Green, and Co.

Johnson, K. E. (1992). The relationship between teachers' beliefs and practices during literacy instruction for non-native speakers of English. *Journal of Reading Behavior, 24*(1), 83–108.

Johnson, K. E. (1994). The emerging beliefs and instructional practices of pre-service ESL teachers. *Teaching and Teacher Education, 10*(4), 439–452.

Johnson, K. E. (2015). Reclaiming the relevance of L2 teacher education. *Modern Language Journal, 99*(3), 515–528.

Kartchava, E., Gatbonton, E., Ammar, A., & Trofimovich, P. (2020). Oral corrective feedback: Pre-service English as a second language teachers' beliefs and practices. *Language Teaching Research, 24*(2), 220–249. https://doi.org/10.1177/1362168818787546

Kinzer, C. K. (1988). Instructional frameworks and instructional choices: Comparisons between preservice and in-service teachers. *Journal of Reading Behavior, 20*(4), 357–377.

Kivunja, C., & Kuyini, A. B. (2017). Understanding and applying research paradigms in educational contexts. *International Journal of Higher Education, 6*(5). https://doi.org/10.5430/ijhe.v6n5p26

Kubanyiova, M., & Feryok, A. (2015). Language teacher cognition in applied linguistics research: Revisiting the territory, redrawing the boundaries, reclaiming the relevance. *The Modern Language Journal, 99*(3), 435–449. https://doi.org/10.1111/modl.12239

Kuhn, T. S. (1962). *The structure of scientific revolutions.* University of Chicago Press.

Lather, P. (1986). Research as praxis. *Harvard Educational Review, 56*(3), 257–277. https://doi.org/10.17763/haer.56.3.bj2h231877069482

Lave, J. (1988). *Cognition in practice: Mind, mathematics, and culture in everyday life.* Cambridge University Press.

LeCompte, M. D., & Schensul, J. J. (1999). *Designing and conducting ethnographic research.* Altamira Press.

Lenski, S. D., Wham, M. A., & Griffey, D. C. (1998). Literacy orientation survey: A survey to clarify teachers' beliefs and practices. *Reading Research and Instruction, 37*(3), 217–236.

Li, L. (2013). The complexity of language teachers' beliefs and practice: One EFL teacher's theories. *The Language Learning Journal, 41*(2), 175–191. https://doi.org/10.1080/09571736.2013.790132

Lincoln, Y. S. (1995). Emerging criteria for quality in qualitative and interpretive research. *Qualitative Inquiry, 1*, 275–289. https://doi.org/10.1177/107780049500100301

Lincoln, Y. S., & Guba, E. G. (Eds.). (1985). *Naturalistic inquiry.* Sage.

Liu, H., Lin, C.-H., & Zhang, D. (2017). Pedagogical beliefs and attitudes toward information and communication technology: A survey of teachers of English as a foreign language in China. *Computer Assisted Language Learning, 30*(8), 745–765. https://doi.org/10.1080/09588221.2017.1347572

Luck, L., Jackson, D., & Usher, K. (2006). Case study: A bridge across the paradigms. *Nursing Inquiry, 13*(2), 103–109.

Mackenzie, N., & Knipe, S. (2006). Research dilemmas: Paradigms, methods and methodology. *Issues in Educational Research, 16*, 1–15.

Markie, P. (2004). Rationalism vs. empiricism. In E. N. Zalta (Ed.), *The Stanford Encyclopedia of Philosophy*. http://plato.stanford.edu/archives/sum2012/entries/rationalism-empiricism

Mercer, S. (2011). Language learner self-concept: Complexity, continuity and change. *System, 39*(3), 335–346.

Merriam, S. (1998). *Qualitative research and case study applications in education*. Jossey-Bass.

Metz, M. (2019). Accommodating linguistic prejudice? Examining English teachers' language ideologies. *English Teaching-Practice and Critique, 18*(1), 18–35. https://doi.org/10.1108/ETPC-09-2018-0081

Meyer, H. D., & Benavot, A. (2013). *PISA, power, and policy: The emergence of global educational governance*. Symposium Books.

Moodie, I., & Feryok, A. (2015). Beyond cognition to commitment: English language teaching in South Korean primary schools. *Modern Language Journal, 99*(3), 450–469.

Murphy, J. (1990). *Pragmatism: From Peirce to Davidson*. Westview Press.

Navarro, D., & Thornton, K. (2011). Investigating the relationship between belief and action in self-directed language learning. *System, 39*(3), 290–301.

Negueruela-Azarola, E. (2011). Beliefs as conceptualizing activity: A dialectical approach for the second language classroom. *System, 39*(3), 359–369.

Nespor, J. (1987). The role of beliefs in the practice of teaching. *Journal of Curriculum Studies, 19*(4), 317–328.

Neuman, W. L. (2011). *Social research methods: Qualitative and quantitative approaches* (7th ed.). Pearson.

Nisbett, R. E., & Wilson, T. D. (1977). Telling more than we can know: Verbal reports on mental processes. *Psychological Review, 84*(3), 231–259.

Pajares, M. F. (1992). Teachers' beliefs and educational research: Cleaning up a messy construct. *Review of Educational Research, 62*(3), 307–332.

Peirce, B. N. (1995). Social identity, investment, and language learning. *TESOL Quarterly, 29*(1), 9–31.

Peng, J. E. (2011). Changes in language learning beliefs during a transition to tertiary study: The mediation of classroom affordances. *System, 39*(3), 314–324.

Phakiti, A., & Plonsky, L. (2018). Reconciling beliefs about L2 learning with SLA theory and research. *RELC Journal, 49*(2), 217–237. https://doi.org/10.1177/0033688218781970

Portoles, L., & Marti, O. (2020). Teachers' beliefs about multilingual pedagogies and the role of initial training. *International Journal of Multilingualism, 17*(2), 248–264. https://doi.org/10.1080/14790718.2018.1515206

Powers, S. W., Zippay, C., & Butler, B. (2006). Investigating connections between teacher beliefs and instructional practices with struggling readers. *Reading Horizons, 47*(2), 121–157.

Pressley, M. (2006). *Reading instruction that works: The case for balanced teaching.* The Guilford Press.

Pressley, M., & Harris, K. (1997). Constructivism and instruction. *Issues in Education, 3*(2), 245–256.

Renandya, W. A. (2007). The power of extensive reading. *RELC Journal, 38*(2), 133–149. https://doi.org/10.1177/0033688207079578

Richardson, V., Anders, P., Tidwell, D., & Lloyd, C. (1991). The relationship between teachers' beliefs and practices in reading comprehension instruction. *American Educational Research Journal, 28*(3), 559–586.

Rosenblatt, L. M. (1986). The literary transaction. In P. Demers (Ed.), *The creating word* (pp. 66–85). Palgrave Macmillan. https://doi.org/10.1007/978-1-349-07954-4_4

Rumelhart, D. E. (1977). Toward an interactive model of reading. In S. Dornic (Ed.), *Attention and performance VI* (pp. 572–603). Laurence Erlbaum Associates.

Rupley, W. H., & Logan, J. W. (1985). Elementary teachers' beliefs about reading and knowledge of reading content: Relationships to decision about reading outcomes. *Reading Psychology, 6*(3–4), 145–156. https://doi.org/10.1080/0270271850060303

Sato, K., & Kleinsasser, R. C. (2004). Beliefs, practices and interactions of teachers in a Japanese high school English department. *Teaching and Teacher Education, 20*(8), 797–816.

Scotland, J. (2012). Exploring the philosophical underpinnings of research: Relating ontology and epistemology to the methodology and methods of the scientific, interpretive, and critical research paradigms. *Teaching, 5*(9), 9–16. https://doi.org/10.5539/elt.v5n9p9

Scott, D., & Usher, R. (2004). *Researching education: Data, methods, and theory in educational enquiry.* Continuum.

Shavelson, R. J., Webb, N. M., & Burstein, L. (1986). Measurement of teaching. In M. C. Wittrock (Eds.), *Handbook of research on teaching* (3rd ed., pp. 50–91). Macmillan.

Smith, F. (1971). *Understanding reading.* Holt, Rinehart & Winston.

Svalberg, A. M. L. (2015). Understanding the complex processes in developing student teachers' knowledge about grammar. *Modern Language Journal, 99*(3), 529–545.

Tashakkori, A., & Teddlie, C. (2003a). *Handbook of mixed methods in social & behavioral research.* Sage.

Tashakkori, A., & Teddlie, C. (2003b). Major issues and controversies in the use of mixed methods in the social and behavioral sciences. In A. Tashakorri & C. Teddlie (Eds.), *Handbook of mixed methods in social & behavioral research* (pp. 3–50). Sage.

Trent, J. (2012). The discursive positioning of teachers: Native-speaking English teachers and educational discourse in Hong Kong. *TESOL Quarterly, 46*(1), 104–126.

van den Broek, E., Oolbekkink-Marchand, H. W., Unsworth, S., van Kemenade, A. M. C., & Meijer, P. C. (2018). Unravelling upper-secondary school teachers' beliefs about language awareness: From conflicts to challenges in the EFL context. *Language Awareness, 27*(4), 331–353. https://doi.org/10.1080/09658416.2018.1523910

van der Schaaf, M. F., Stokking, K. M., & Verloop, N. (2008). Teacher beliefs and teacher behaviour in portfolio assessment. *Teaching and Teacher Education, 24*(7), 1691–1704. https://doi.org/10.1016/j.tate.2008.02.021

van Geert, P. (2011), The contribution of complex dynamic systems to development. *Child Development Perspectives, 5*(4), 273–278. https://doi.org/10.1111/j.1750-8606.2011.00197.x

Wilson, E. K., Konopak, B. C., & Readence, J. E. (1993). Examining content area reading beliefs, decisions, and instruction: A case study of an English teacher. In C. Kinzer & D. Leu (Eds.), *Forty-first yearbook of the National Reading Conference.* National Reading Conference.

Woods, D., & Cakir, H. (2011). Two dimensions of teacher knowledge: The case of communicative language teaching. *System, 39*(3), 381–390.

Yang, J. S., & Kim, T. Y. (2011). Sociocultural analysis of second language learner beliefs: A qualitative case study of two study-abroad ESL learners. *System, 39*(3), 325–334.

Yin, R. K. (2003). *Case study research: Design and methods.* Sage.

Zainal, Z. (2003). Critical review of reading model and theories in first and second language. *Human Journal/Jurnal Kemanusiaan, 1*(2), 104–124.

Zheng, H. (2015). *Teacher beliefs as a complex system: English language teachers in China.* Springer International. https://doi.org/10.1007/978-3-319-23009-2

Complex Dynamic Systems Theory as a Theoretical Framework to Study Beliefs and Practice of EFL Reading Teachers

1   Introduction

In the previous chapter, I presented how different epistemological, ontological, methodological, and axiological beliefs and underpinnings have informed the change of research paradigms over the decades. I ended that chapter by arguing the complicated, ever-changing issues of the world have fueled the emergence of pragmatism, a paradigm that attempts to analyze, interpret, and solve today's complex problems. Taking teacher beliefs and practice as an example, tensions between these beliefs and their actual practice are far more complex than we expected. These tensions might be caused by different factors from personal, institutional, and sociocultural contexts.

Aligning the pragmatist research paradigm with suitable theoretical frameworks is necessary and helpful for teachers and researchers. In this chapter, I provide a general picture of how complex dynamic systems theory (CDST) can be used as a suitable theoretical framework for studying teacher belief systems and also how it connects with a practice system. I also discuss and present methodological steps, procedures, and issues in studying teacher beliefs and practices of EFL reading teachers from a CDST perspective.

2   Introducing Complex Dynamic Systems Theory

It is challenging (and maybe even impossible) to give a full account of the origin of the term *complex theory*, as the term *complex* itself is extensively found in different disciplines as a canonical tenet. Some scholars (e.g., Martin et al., 2019) would argue that complex theory was originally taken from physics when in 1948 Warren Weaver introduced a number of terms from the discipline, including *simple systems*, *disorganized complex systems*, and *organized complexity*, as the prototypic terms describing the theory. Others (e.g., Larsen-Freeman & Cameron, 2008) took a mathematical perspective and traced the origin of the terminology to classic writings by Henri Poincaré in 1889. The theory evolved quickly during the 1950s and the 1960s by including tenets or insights from chaos theory, quantum physics, evolutionary biology, system theory, chemistry, cybernetics, artificial intelligence, economics, and organizational management (Cochran-Smith et al., 2014; Feryok, 2010).

Many still argue about the origins of the official terms used within and the proper title of the theory, which includes (but is not limited to) *complex theory, dynamic system theory, complex system theory*, and *CDST*. All have been used interchangeably over the years. The evolution of the terms from complex theory to CDST in a way indicates the accrual of tenets and fine-grained attributes of the theory; however, selection of a specific term may depend on the specific discipline. I prefer the term *CDST*, which is more often used in educational settings, in social science studies (Koopmans & Stamovlasis, 2016), and typically in applied linguistics (Larsen-Freeman, 2019); it directly represents what the theory indicates and includes complex, dynamic, and systemic attributes of a certain phenomenon. Martin, McQuitty, and Morgan (2019) further argued that the theory is a learning theory that attempts to address key attributes in complex systems, including "self-organization, emergence, nested, dynamic and far from equilibrium, difficulty to predict outcomes, interactions, ambiguously bounded, and feedback loops" (pp. 3–4). These attributes, again, echo the primary nature of the complex systems which are agentive, adaptive, complex, dynamic, emergent, and evolving.

CDST has been, while not extensively, applied to social science and educational studies, including cognitive development (e.g., Thelen & Smith, 1993), applied linguistics and second language development (de Bot et al., 2007; Larsen-Freeman, 1997, 2002; Larsen-Freeman & Cameron, 2008; van Lier, 1998, 2004), and teacher education (e.g., Koopmans & Stamovlasis, 2016; Steenbeek & van Geert, 2013; van Geert & Steenbeek, 2005a, 2005b). For example, from a CDST perspective, a group of scholastic works (e.g., de Bot et al., 2013; Larsen-Freeman, 1997) in second language acquisition made a fundamental contribution to the field by advocating a change from *acquisition* to *development*, from a *static* language-learning process to an *evolving, constantly changing* process. Central to these applications stands the idea that different components of a system interact in particular ways to produce an overall state (Larsen-Freeman & Cameron, 2008). However, empirical studies are still far less developed than conceptual works.

3 Complex Dynamic Systems Theory and the Pragmatism Paradigm

As discussed in the previous chapter, pragmatism focuses on real-world problems that are too complicated to be solved by applying a single paradigm.

Pragmatism does not require researchers to generate a universal solution to a single problem, but instead leads them to identify and analyze the actual situations in which all factors are interconnected to create a complex picture.

The paradigm of pragmatism is not committed to any specific philosophy or reality, but instead to the complexity of real-world problems (Cherryholmes, 1992; Murphy, 1990). Scholars and researchers using the pragmatism paradigm acknowledge the existence of divergences, inconsistencies, and barriers in social, historical, political, and other contexts. For example, the pragmatism paradigm works great as an embodiment in the studies of EFL teachers' beliefs and practices when researchers attempt to identify teachers' beliefs as a complex system (Barcelos & Kalaja, 2011).

Under the premise that a teacher's belief system is complex and even more complex when being interwoven with the teacher's practice, I attempt to look for a suitable theoretical framework to be aligned with the pragmatism paradigm. CDST, therefore, emerges as the chosen one. Instead of looking at the world through simple cause-and-effect models, linear predictability and separate constructs and entities, CDST views the world as an organic, nonlinear and holistic system in which subsystems coevolve and interact with each other to sustain the development of their own. In other words, epistemological and ontological assumptions behind CDST regard the phenomenon of interest as a complex dynamic system – "The dynamic interactive relationship between Chinese secondary school EFL teachers' beliefs and practice" (Hilpert & Marchand, 2018; Kaplan et al., 2012) – and understand the phenomenon as embedded in a hierarchy of systems, one that is nested in a larger system and is constituted by elements that are subsystems. The very nature of CDST fits well with the epistemological and ontological beliefs of the pragmatism which acknowledge the existence of divergences, inconsistencies, and barriers in social, historical, political, and other contexts. Each construct or context may be seen as a subsystem, informing or restricting the development of another construct or context.

4   Complex Dynamic Systems Theory in Educational Settings

Many studies in educational settings have been conducted through a CDST lens. One of the features of these studies is that researchers often set up dyad constructs that could coevolve as the focal points of the studies. For example, Steenbeek and van Geert (2013) studied the emergence of the learning-teaching trajectory from a CDST perspective. Quite a few dyads were examined in their study, including the learning and teaching dyad, the student and teacher dyad, and the successful and unsuccessful trajectory dyad. Specifically, they analyzed successful and unsuccessful learning-teaching trajectories as emergent and dynamic phenomena resulting from the interactions in the entire educational context.

In particular, Steenbeek and van Geert (2013) examined the learning-teaching trajectories as processes that a student and a teacher self-regulated, other-regulated, and coregulated. They specifically proposed two dynamic models: one on the short-term dynamics of learning-teaching interactions in classrooms and the other on the long-term dynamics of interactions in a network of variables encompassing concerns, evaluations, actions, and action effects between students and teachers. With their attempts and contribution, the learning-teaching trajectory which used to be analyzed through a static, psychological lens became dynamic and modalized through a complex, coadaptive system.

The findings from Steenbeek and van Geert (2013) offered great insights for the current study on EFL reading teachers' beliefs and practice. Teachers' beliefs include their learning and prior knowledge learned; their practice is their actual teaching. The learning and teaching dyad can thus be further explored and analyzed through the CDST perspective. However, as a continuation of their previous studies (van Geert & Steenbeek, 2005a, 2005b, 2007; van Geert, 2008), Steenbeek and van Geert (2013) depicted their models through differential equations and in primarily a quantitative way. This is not the primary way I present the findings of the current study.

5   Complex Dynamic Systems Theory in Language Education

As mentioned earlier in this chapter, Larsen-Freeman was the first of a group of scholars in applied linguistics and TESOL who adopted CDST as a theoretical lens to study language acquisition and language development. Larsen-Freeman (2019) provided a historical account on the development of linguistics and linguistic studies. She started with a simplistic linguistic debate when the behaviorist view that linguistics as simply a systemic study of rule-based language units was challenged by Chomsky's cognitive view that language learners' intuitive knowledge of a specific language guides them to learn and speak that language. Then, she elaborated on how a psycholinguistic process represented by Selinker (1972) offered insights into theories such as processability (Pienemann, 1998), input processing (van Patten, 1996), and skill acquisition (DeKeyser, 1998). She further summarized how anthropology, sociology and the most recent cognitive theories broadened the scope of linguistic studies and offered more explanatory insights into it. With this historical account, she showed the necessity of the transdisciplinary lens with CDST to be the representative theory, and issued a call for it.

More specifically, Larsen-Freeman (2019) promoted the advocacy of CDST as a way to compensate for and replace a reductionist way of thinking. As an interdisciplinary theory, CDST highlights the dynamic, variable, nonlinear nature of second language development, which echoes an ecological conception of development. One of the most important, Larsen-Freeman argued, is from a CDST perspective: second language development is "not a matter of input becoming output, but rather that language patterns emerge from the interaction of its users, given the affordances that they perceive" (p. 267). She concluded the article with a discussion of several instructional implications from a CDST perspective.

While Larsen-Freeman (1997) made a contribution by proposing tenets in complex theory to the language education field, scholars using the theoretical framework yielded fruits in *quantity* rather than *quality*, particularly in the 2010s. Most of the works are more conceptual than empirical, more about *talking* than *doing* (Dörnyei et al., 2014). As part of the belief system in the current study is the reading beliefs which were closely looked into from a linguistic perspective, I attempted to address the gap and join the existing literature.

6   Complex Dynamic Systems Theory in EFL Reading Studies

Zheng Hongying (2013b) adopted CDST to explore the features of the teachers' belief system and how interactions among different components of the belief system account for the attributes of the system. Zheng conducted a case study with an English teacher in a Chinese secondary school and used the methods of semi-structured interviews, observations, and stimulated recall interviews to reveal the coexistence of different beliefs. She also found the interactions among these beliefs determined the relationship between the teacher's beliefs and practice. She argued that tensions between teacher beliefs and actual practices might be accounted for from "token adoption," an eclectic approach that helped the teacher with interpreting her inconsistency between beliefs and practices during any curriculum reform.

Zheng (2013b) paved the way for studies on EFL teacher beliefs and confirmed that they mapped out a dynamic, nonlinear system which could interact with teacher practices in one way or another. More importantly, in her other works (e.g., Zheng, 2013a, 2015), she created a general picture of how the Chinese EFL context differs from other contexts and provided either favorable or limited affordances to language teachers. However, Zheng's works primarily utilized a single case study, the analysis of which, while qualitative in nature, provided a limited contribution to a larger range of audiences or teachers in diversified contexts. In addition, while Zheng focused on the language teacher in the Chinese EFL context, she treated her participant Li as a language teacher who taught across different language skills instead of simply focusing on the reading skill.

The current study drew upon Zheng's works (e.g., 2013a, 2013b, 2015) for the context and belief system analyses. However, it differed greatly from the existing literature in the way that it focused on a wider body of participants and specific reading and reading teaching beliefs. The mixed-methods approach in the current study also deepened the analysis of the belief and practice constructs. What's more, the current study spent a few sections elaborating on specific theoretical orientations to reading which served as reading teachers' prior knowledge of the content area and informed their beliefs of teaching reading. The fine-grained analyses of reading orientations, reading beliefs, and teaching beliefs made the current study unique and significant. The above literature review on how CDST has been applied to educational studies, language linguistics, and EFL teacher education provides a foundational framework for the current study.

7   Steps in Conducting the Study with a CDST Lens

Kaplan and Garner (2020) contributed a proposed framework for applying CDST in educational research. Taking into account ontological, theoretical, and methodological principles and underpinnings, they suggested six interdependent steps for researchers who seek to pursue educational research from a CDST perspective:

1.   Conceptualizing the phenomenon as a CDS
2.   Defining a theory of the relevant CDS level
3.   Generating a CDS research goal and questions
4.   Selecting a CDS corresponding methodology for data collection and analysis
5.   Interpreting the findings as a CDS
6.   Disseminating the knowledge to relevant audiences and participating in a CDS scholarly community (Kaplan & Garner, 2020, p. 1).

While the fine-grained steps provided the reader with a clear picture of how CDST studies can be conducted, some of the steps seem so generic that they can be applied to any type of research. Therefore, I studied the given steps and made the necessary adaptations. One big challenge to the application of the six steps to the current study is the fact that Kaplan and Garner (2020) regarded CDS as a paradigmatic approach instead of a theoretical framework. They believed specific theories (including sociocognitive theory and sociocultural theory) may work as specific theoretical frameworks to support the paradigmatic approach. Therefore, they identified Step 2 as *defining a theory of the relevant CDS level* among all the given steps. This may not be working in the current study, as I as well as some other scholars (e.g., Larsen-Freeman, 2019) treated CDST as a transdisciplinary theory. This distinction between the paradigmatic approach and the theoretical framework meant that the application of the steps required adaptation. However, the adaptation did exclude Step 2, as I agreed with some tenets in the elaboration on the step. I thus drew upon the resonating tenets and reframed the step as *identifying the constructs and dynamics studied in the CDST phenomenon.*

Another point that might be improved or adapted is Step 3. While Kaplan and Garner (2020) believed *generating a research goal and questions* to be a necessary step in CDST studies, it overlaps with conceptualizing a CDST phenomenon. Research goals and questions can be seen as necessities in the conceptualization of a phenomenon. In the remainder of this section, I provide the reader with detailed explanations of the adapted steps as well as analyses on how the current study had been conducted in the adapted steps. I also end the chapter with the implications of how studies in the future might be improved in terms of their design and experimental procedures.

Kaplan and Garner (2020) argued that conceptualizing a phenomenon from the CDST perspective involves questions and assumptions looking into "the nature and recurring patterns of the system's emergent behavior" (p. 2). They further explained *time scale*, *boundary conditions*, and *possible phases* for these recurring patterns may all be good focal points to support the conceptualization of a certain CDST phenomenon. For example, Pennings and Hollenstein (2020) conceptualized teacher-student relationships as a CDST phenomenon and presented the behavior in moment-to-moment interactions. Their analysis interpreted the behavior from a micro-level and depicted recurring patterns in hourly or daily time scales. This resembles what Steenbeek and van Geert (2013) offered as the short-time dynamics of the learning and teaching trajectory.

As mentioned earlier, one of the primary differences between the six steps in Kaplan and Garner (2020) and the steps proposed in the current study is the distinction between a paradigmatic view and a theoretical view of treating CDS. As I prefer to regard CDS as a theoretical framework, I agreed with other scholars (e.g., Larsen-Freeman, 2019) to put a T after CDS, thus making CDST prevalent in the study. Therefore, Step 2 in Kaplan and Garner (2020) was adapted for the study. I agreed with Kaplan and Garner (2020) in elaborating on the step to explicate primary system facets, including system elements and structure, the dynamic formation of the elements and the emergent process, and the conditions and factors. I thus adapted the step and named it as *identifying the constructs and dynamics studied in the CDST phenomenon*. For example, in the current study, the teacher belief system is one of the primary constructs to be studied. It may include different subsystems of the beliefs, i.e., a belief system of theoretical orientation to reading and a belief system of teaching reading. Dynamics may refer to the ever-changing dyadic interactions between belief subsystems and the belief-practice system. Factors may include personal, institutional, and sociocultural factors which may either facilitate or restrict the evolution of the system.

Specifically, the personal factors may include psychological constructs, e.g., the identity and agency of EFL teachers; the institutional factors may be school policies, required curriculum design, and assigned teaching and/or research load; sociocultural factors may include cultural, ideological, and political constraints (Gao, 2020, 2021a, 2021b). All these factors may either impede or inform the consistency between beliefs and practices. For example, a female teacher who is also a young mother may hold a multiple but unbalanced identity system when she puts being a mother ahead of her other identities, including being a teacher and a wife. She might attempt to teach as she believed and meant to teach, but then just couldn't complete the instruction due to her maternal responsibilities. She believed that multimodality helps improve her teaching and her students' understanding of the content area knowledge and thus wanted to prepare a number of multimodal tasks for her class; however, she had to end the preparation due to a scheduled pick-up of her daughter. Or, the teacher may attempt to implement a multimodal curriculum design in her class but finally abandoned the design when her school required teachers to focus more on the instruction of test-prep skills rather than the engagement of the students. Identifying these elements and factors informs the development and implementation of the current study.

As discussed in the previous chapter, research paradigms offer insights into the selection of research methodologies, as they provide the methodologies with epistemological and ontological underpinnings that fit the use of the methodologies and make them the best instruments or weapons to explore a certain phenomenon. As CDST studies primarily explore nonlinear, complex relationships among different systems or constructs, quantitative methods in a positivist paradigm to prove a certain, unidirectional relationship among constructs are thus not suitable for a typical CDST study. Qualitative methods in an interpretivist or constructivist paradigm are better than simple quantitative methods to explore dynamics in depth. For example, Koopmans (2020) suggested ethnographic methods in educational settings are desirable and suitable for CDST studies, as they are helpful in exploring and depicting nuanced interactions among different systems in a scalar approach. However, it is worth mentioning that CDST studies in educational settings or social science studies do not reject the use of quantitative methodologies. Quantitative methodologies remain helpful in presenting the relationships of the subsystems and exploring the nested structure of the holistic system, which fits part of the very nature of the CDST phenomenon. Therefore, mixed-methods approaches fit methodological requirements in typical CDST studies.

This study adopted an exploratory sequential design based on mixed-methods design classifications (Creswell et al., 2003). When choosing the research method, I focused on whether the design fit my research questions. Choosing an appropriate mixed-methods design requires the consideration of three issues: priority, implementation, and integration (Creswell et al., 2003). Priority refers to what specific approach – the quantitative or the qualitative – is given more emphasis. Priority is closely connected with the types of research questions – whether researchers want to investigate "what" and "how" in qualitative studies or "if" in quantitative studies. Then, implementation determines the sequence of data collection, i.e., whether the quantitative and qualitative data collection and analysis come in sequence or in parallel. Integration occurs when researchers strive to mix or connect the data after the data collection in the research process.

Kaplan and Garner (2020) argued that

> when investigating a phenomenon conceptualized as a CDS, the methodology would optimally involve collection and analysis of data that capture all facets of the target system: its elements, their relations, their change, and the external and internal conditions and factors that frame the system's emergence and their change. (p. 3)

The present study showed exploratory and sequential features in addressing these issues. For the exploratory feature, the primary purpose (priority) of the study is to explore the characteristics of the stated belief system about reading and teaching reading, and also to examine and report the relationships or interactions between stated beliefs and actual practices among the teachers. To fulfill the research purposes, it does take steps and procedures which bring about a multilayered study with qualitative data collected and analyzed first, and then quantified in numeric codes (integration). While the discussion of the study is centered around the possible constraints that caused inconsistencies between beliefs and practices, the exploration of the characteristics and inconsistencies was the priority. The use of quantitative data in the study was consistent with the sequential exploratory design, in which the quantitative component assists in the interpretation of qualitative findings (Creswell et al., 2003).

Kaplan and Garner (2020) further argued that interpreting the data in CDST studies should serve two primary functions: first, interpretations of the data should cater to provide rich information on how different faceted elements or constructs map out the general system; second, interpretations of the data should also offer implications to theory, research, and policy. In this study, I described the findings of the study in connection with the three research questions. Theoretically, I presented how reading orientations, together with teaching beliefs about these orientations, among EFL teachers interweaved to form a complex belief system. Practically, how teachers adhered in the belief system may or may not inform their actual practices in the classroom, which indicated a nonlinear relationship between beliefs and practices.

8   Conceptual Frameworks

A conceptual framework helps researchers with systems of theories, concepts, assumptions, and beliefs that are used to inform the design of their research (Maxwell, 2005; Miles & Huberman, 1994; Robson, 2002). A conceptual framework covers three constructs. First, it helps researchers identify the *theoretical perspective* they use to develop their research, test their research hypotheses, and interpret their research data. Second, it helps researchers map out the *process* of doing their research, the specific stages that their research may go through, and how they connect one stage with another. This relates to the research design, which helps researchers prove how they can carry out the research. The last construct is the *research paradigm*, which relates to a researcher's epistemology and ontology and is used to explain both what the researcher thinks the knowledge is and how he/she thinks knowledge can be formed. For example, if a researcher's paradigm is rooted in positivism, he/she will probably use a quantitative design to conduct his/her research. However, the three constructs in a conceptual framework are not clear-cut; they often overlap or are embedded within one another (see Figure 2).

Therefore, the conceptual framework is determined by the research method used. As this study is mixed-methods, it adopts a pragmatism paradigm which

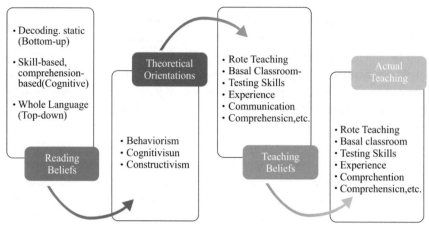

FIGURE 2   Conceptual framework of teachers' beliefs and practices

includes both quantitative and qualitative designs. A quantitative design entails features of positivism, and a qualitative design primarily entails design features of constructivism, particularly for the socio-constructivism in the study. To be more specific, the positivism paradigm is used to investigate the inconsistency or consistency between teachers' beliefs and their practices and to review the literature on this topic. In addition, the constructivism paradigm is used to examine the relationship between beliefs and practices from a dynamic and complex perspective instead of a single and static one.

References

Barcelos, A. M. F., & Kalaja, P. (2011). Introduction to beliefs about SLA revisited. *System, 39*(3), 281–289.

Cherryholmes, C. (1992). Notes on pragmatism and scientific realism. *Educational Researcher, 21*(6), 13–17.

Cochran-Smith, M., Ell, F., Ludlow, L., Grudnoff, L., & Aitken, G. (2014). The challenge and promise of complexity theory for teacher education research. *Teachers College Record, 116*(5), 1–38.

Creswell, J. W., Plano Clark, V. L., Gutmann, M. L., & Hanson, W. E. (2003). Advanced mixed methods research designs. In A. Tashakkori & C. Teddlie (Eds.), *Handbook on mixed methods in the behavioral and social sciences* (pp. 209–240). Sage.

de Bot, K., Lowie, W., Thorne, S. L., & Verspoor, M. H. (2013). Dynamic systems theory as a comprehensive theory of second language development. In M. P. García Mayo, M. J. Gutiérrez Mangado, & M. Martínez-Adrián (Eds.), *Contemporary perspectives on second language acquisition* (pp. 167–189). John Benjamins. https://doi.org/10.1075/aals.9.13ch10

de Bot, K., Lowie, W., & Verspoor, M. (2007). A dynamic systems theory approach to second language acquisition. *Bilingualism: Language and Cognition, 10*, 7–21. https://doi.org/10.1017/S1366728906002732

DeKeyser, R. M. (1998). Beyond focus on form: Cognitive perspectives on learning and practicing second language grammar. In C. Doughty & J. Williams (Eds.), *Focus on form in classroom second language acquisition* (pp. 42–63). Cambridge University Press.

Dörnyei, Z., MacIntyre, P. D., & Henry, A. (2014). Introduction: Applying Complex Dynamic Systems Principles to Empirical Research on L2 Motivation: In Z. Dörnyei, P. D. MacIntyre, & A. Henry (Eds.), *Motivational dynamics in language learning* (pp. 1–7). Multilingual Matters. https://doi.org/doi:10.21832/9781783092574-003

Feryok, A. (2010). Language teacher cognitions: Complex dynamic systems? *System: An International Journal of Educational Technology and Applied Linguistics, 38*(2), 272–279.

Gao, Y. (2019). Teaching technical communication to engineering students: Design, implementation, and assessment for project-based instruction. In *Proceedings of the Interdisciplinary STEM Teaching and Learning Conference* (Vol. 3, Article 6, pp. 77–87). https://doi.org/10.20429/stem.2019.030106

Gao, Y. (2020). How transnational experiences and political, economic policies inform transnational intellectuals' identities and mobility: An autoethnographic study. *Higher Education Policy.* https://doi.org/10.1057/s41307-020-00187-w

Gao, Y. (2021a). How do language learning, teaching, and transnational experiences (Re)shape an EFLer's identities? A critical ethnographic narrative. *SAGE Open, 11*(3), https://doi.org/10.1177/21582440211031211

Gao, Y., & Zhou, Y. (2021b). Exploring language teachers' beliefs about the medium of instruction and actual practices using complex dynamic system theory. *Frontiers in Education, 6*, 708031. https://doi.org/10.3389/feduc.2021.708031

Hilpert, J. C., & Marchand, G. C. (2018). Complex systems research in educational psychology: Aligning theory and method. *Educational Psychologist, 53*(3), 185–202. https://doi.org/10.1080/00461520.2018.1469411

Kaplan, A., & Garner, J. K. (2020). Steps for applying the complex dynamical systems approach in educational research: A guide for the perplexed scholar. *The Journal of Experimental Education, 88*(3), 486–502. https://doi.org/10.1080/00220973.2020.1745738

Kaplan, A., Katz, I., & Flum, H. (2012). Motivation theory in educational practice: Knowledge claims, challenges, and future directions. In *APA educational psychology handbook, vol. 2: Individual differences and cultural and contextual factors* (pp. 165–194). American Psychological Association. https://doi.org/10.1037/13274-007

Koopmans, M. (2020). Education is a complex dynamical system: Challenges for research. *The Journal of Experimental Education, 88*(3), 358–374. https://doi.org/10.1080/00220973.2019.1566199

Koopmans, M., & Stamovlasis, D. (2016). *Complex dynamical systems in education.* Springer International Publishing. https://doi.org/10.1007/978-3-319-27577-2

Larsen-Freeman, D. (1997). Chaos/complexity science and second language acquisition. *Applied Linguistics, 18*(2), 141–165.

Larsen-Freeman, D. (2002). Language acquisition and language use from a chaos/complexity theory perspective. In C. Kramsch (Ed.), *Language acquisition and socialization* (pp. 33–46). Continuum.

Larsen-Freeman, D. (2019). Second language development in its time: Expanding our scope of inquiry. *Chinese Journal of Applied Linguistics, 42*(3), 267–284. https://doi.org/10.1515/CJAL-2019-0017

Larsen-Freeman, D., & Cameron, L. (2008). Research methodology on language development from a complex systems perspective. *The Modern Language Journal, 92*(2), 200–213.

Martin, S. D., McQuitty, V., & Morgan, D. N. (2019, March 26). Complexity theory and teacher education. In *Oxford research encyclopedia of education.* https://doi.org/10.1093/acrefore/9780190264093.013.479

Maxwell, J. A. (2005). *Qualitative research design: An interactive approach* (2nd ed.). Sage.

Miles, M. B., & Huberman, A. M. (1994). *Qualitative data analysis* (2nd ed.). Sage.

Morse, J. M. (1994). Designing funded qualitative research. In N. K. Denizin & Y. S. Lincoln (Eds.), *Handbook of qualitative research* (2nd ed., pp. 220–235). Sage.

Murphy, J. (1990). *Pragmatism: From Peirce to Davidson.* Westview Press.

Pennings, H. J. M., & Hollenstein, T. (2020). Teacher-student interactions and teacher interpersonal styles: A state space grid analysis. *Journal of Experimental Education, 88*(3), 382–406. https://doi.org/10.1080/00220973.2019.1578724

Pienemann, M. (1998). *Language processing and second language development: Processability theory.* John Benjamins. https://doi.org/10.1075/sibil.15

Robson, C. (2002). *Real world research: A resource for social scientists and practitioner researchers.* Blackwell.

Selinker. (1972). Interlanguage. *International Review of Applied Linguistics in Language Teaching, 10*(3), 209–241.

Steenbeek, H., & van Geert, P. (2013). The emergence of learning-teaching trajectories in education: A complex dynamic systems approach. *Nonlinear Dynamics, Psychology, and Life Sciences, 17*(2), 233–267.

Steenbeek, H. W., & van Geert, P. L. C. (2007). A theory and dynamic model of dyadic interaction: Concerns, appraisals, and contagiousness in a developmental context. *Developmental Review, 27*(1), 1–40. https://doi.org/10.1016/j.dr.2006.06.002

Thelen, E., & Smith, L. B. (1993). *A dynamic systems approach to the development of cognition and action* (new ed.). MIT Press.

van Geert, P. (2008). The dynamic systems approach in the study of L1 and L2 acquisition: An introduction. *The Modern Language Journal, 92*(2), 179–199. https://onlinelibrary.wiley.com/doi/abs/10.1111/j.1540-4781.2008.00713.x

van Geert, P., & Steenbeek, H. (2005a). The dynamics of scaffolding. *New Ideas in Psychology, 23*(3), 115–128. https://doi.org/10.1016/j.newideapsych.2006.05.003

van Geert, P., & Steenbeek, H. (2005b). Explaining after by before: Basic aspects of a dynamic systems approach to the study of development. *Developmental Review, 25*(3–4), 408–442.

van Lier, L. (1998). The relationship between consciousness, interaction, and language learning. *Language Awareness, 7*, 128–143.

van Lier, L. (2004). *The ecology and semiotics of language learning: A sociocultural perspective*. Kluwer.

van Patten, B. (1996). *Input processing and grammar instruction in second language acquisition*. Praeger.

Zheng, H. (2013a). The dynamic interactive relationship between Chinese secondary school EFL teachers' beliefs and practice. *The Language Learning Journal, 41*(2), 192–204. https://doi.org/10.1080/09571736.2013.790133

Zheng, H. (2013b). Teachers' beliefs and practices: A dynamic and complex relationship. *Asia-Pacific Journal of Teacher Education, 41*(3), 331–343. https://doi.org/10.1080/1359866X.2013.809051

Zheng, H. (2015). *Teacher beliefs as a complex system: English language teachers in China*. Springer International. https://doi.org/10.1007/978-3-319-23009-2

Characteristics of Chinese Teachers' Belief Systems

1 An Overview of the Chapter

In the previous chapter, I mapped out the existing literature on language teacher beliefs and practices, particularly in regard to how paradigm shifts have informed the development of related studies. I presented a general picture of how the evolution of ontology, epistemology, theoretical orientations, and methodological approaches to the related studies has developed over the decades and ended up with the conclusion that current research exists within a pragmatist paradigm and that complex dynamic systems theory (CDST) might be suitable to explore language teacher beliefs and practices. With that premise, I have attempted to design a mixed-method study to explore the topic further. As reported in the previous chapter, a pragmatist paradigm entails studies using a mixed-methods design, which takes steps and follows procedures to solve real-world problems. Therefore, in this chapter I take the first step by presenting data and analysis of reading teachers' stated beliefs and describe these beliefs in a quantitative, detailed way. Through a detailed description of their belief systems, I aim to answer the following question: What are the characteristics of Chinese EFL teachers' beliefs about reading and teaching reading? In the end, I conceptualize and visualize the belief systems based on all the data descriptions and the summary of the characteristics.

2 Characteristics of Chinese EFL Teachers' Beliefs about English Reading and Teaching Reading

The findings of the study showed that three theoretical orientations to reading (behaviorism, cognitivism, and constructivism) were matrixed with three different subbelief systems. Specifically, teachers hold different, mixed orientations. The three distinct subbelief systems in the analysis were operationally defined as *dominant, dual,* and *multiple* (Johnson, 1992). The matrix indicated a complex belief system about reading and teaching reading among these EFL teachers.

First, multiple reading orientations coexist in the participants' belief systems. Instead of holding just a single, unique reading orientation, most of the teachers held diverse and multiple orientations – for example, simultaneously being oriented toward behaviorism and cognitivism.

© KONINKLIJKE BRILL NV, LEIDEN, 2022 | DOI: 10.1163/9789004506541_005

Second, these Chinese EFL teachers' reading beliefs and theoretical orientations varied from person to person. An even distribution among the three reading belief systems or orientations was not found. Among the three theoretical orientations to reading, i.e., behaviorism, cognitivism, and constructivism, teachers holding a behaviorism orientation occupy most of the sample. Table 3 illustrates how complexity was presented as a major characteristic in the Chinese EFL teachers' belief systems.

2.1 *Complexity of the Reading Teachers' Belief Systems*

Reading teachers in the study held different reading beliefs, which includes dominant, dual, and multiple belief subsystems. These subsystems were interwoven and coexisted in the overall belief system, causing the system to be complex. A *dominant* reading belief system represents only one theoretical orientation. It resembles what Borg (2003, 2006, 2009) terms as a core belief. Teachers with a dominant belief system occupied 29.2% of the quantitative sample; "behaviorism orientation" was the most commonly coded, with 88 occurrences out of the total 485 (18.1%). Beliefs that fell under dominant constructivism or cognitivism reading orientations accounted for less than 10% of the whole sample, at 7.2% (35 occurrences) and 3.9% (19 occurrences), respectively.

A *dual* belief system stands for the mixture of two theoretical orientations to reading. A matrix with the three potential pairs of dual theoretical orientations was indicated in the study: behaviorism and cognitivism (1 & 2); cognitivism and constructivism (2 & 3); and behaviorism and constructivism (1 & 3). Generally speaking, teachers holding a dual theoretical orientation to reading of any kind accounted for the largest percentage of the entire sample (38.8%), which was almost 10% more than those holding dominant reading belief systems. Teachers holding both behaviorist and constructivist reading beliefs accounted for 17.5% of the participants. Teachers holding both behaviorist and cognitivist reading beliefs accounted for 15.3% of the sample. Teachers with dual cognitivist and constructivist reading beliefs accounted for less than 6% of all the teachers involved in the study. Teachers holding all three reading belief systems, which was operationally defined as a *multiple* theoretical orientation, accounted for 11.1% of all the teachers surveyed (see Table 3).

Similar to the theoretical reading orientations, teachers' stated beliefs about teaching reading were also defined into *dominant, dual,* and *multiple* teaching orientation. A *dominant* teaching reading orientation corresponds to only one single reading belief system. However, different from reading beliefs, teachers holding a dominant teaching belief system occupied the largest percent of the sample (37.8%). The behaviorists made up the largest group of the entire

TABLE 3   Basic descriptive statistics of the belief matrix

Theoretical orientations		Reading beliefs		Teaching beliefs	
Type	Rep.#	Frequency	Percent	Frequency	Percent
Dominant	1	88	18.1	95	19.6
Dual	1, 2	85	17.5	59	12.2
Multiple	1, 2, 3	54	11.1	50	10.3
Dual	1, 3	74	15.3	68	14.0
Dominant	2	36	7.3	31	6.4
Dual	2, 3	29	6.0	18	3.7
Dominant	3	19	3.9	57	11.8
	Missing	101	20.8	107	22.1
	Total	485	100.0	485	100.0

Notes: 1: Behaviorism; 2: Cognitivism; 3: Constructivism
       Dominant: single theoretical orientation; Dual: two theoretical orientations; Multiple:
       all three theoretical orientations

participant pool (19.6%) and were followed by constructivists (11.8%). Only 6.4% of teachers exhibited a cognitivist orientation (see Table 3).

A matrix with three pairs of *dual* theoretical orientations to teaching reading were also indicated in the study: behaviorism and cognitivism (1 & 2); cognitivism and constructivism (2 & 3); and behaviorism and constructivism (1 & 3). Teachers holding dual theoretical orientations occupied 29.9% of the entire sample. To be more specific, teachers holding both behaviorist and constructivist reading beliefs accounted for 14.0% of participants. Teachers holding both behaviorist and cognitivist teaching beliefs made up 12.2% of the study population, while teachers with both cognitivist and constructivist reading beliefs made up less than 4%. Teachers holding a *multiple* belief system which included all three theoretical orientations accounted for 10.3% of all participants (see Table 3).

2.2   *Nonlinearity and Unpredictability of the Subsystem Correspondence*
In addition to the complex coexistence of different theoretical orientations, findings of the study indicated that relationships among different beliefs were nonlinear and unpredictable. For example, one unpredictability occurred in theoretical orientations. Specifically, statistical percentages of a certain belief system did not necessarily indicate similar percentages of the belief system in

TABLE 4   Condensed descriptive statistics of the matrix

	Reading beliefs	Teaching beliefs
Dominant	143	183
	(29.3%)	(37.8%)
Dual	188	135
	(38.8%)	(29.9%)
Multiple	54	50
	(11.1%)	(10.3%)

teaching and vice versa. Table 4 illustrates how unpredictability was presented as another major characteristic in Chinese EFL teachers' belief systems.

Specifically, the largest percentage in reading beliefs was the dual belief system (38.8%), whereas the largest percentage in reading teaching beliefs was the single, behaviorist belief system (37.8%). Likewise, the second largest percentage in reading beliefs was the dominant belief system (29.3%), whereas the second largest percentage in teaching beliefs was not the dominant but the dual belief system (29.9%). It was only the multiple belief system that showed a consistency between its reading belief percentage and its teaching belief percentage.

Likewise, qualitative findings indicated that having one orientation in reading and teaching beliefs was not a significant predictor of which orientation the teacher might hold in actual practice. For example, both S and L held cognitivist reading and teaching beliefs in their survey responses. However, they did not indicate the cognitivist orientation in their actual practices. This kind of unpredictability will be presented and explained in the qualitative findings of Research Questions 2 and 3.

2.2.1   Feature Analysis of the Reading Beliefs

The following section lists qualitative excerpts from the open-ended surveys that provide further insight into the nature of the teachers' theoretical reading orientations. Harste and Burke (1977) stated that "theoretical orientation is best thought of as a cognitivist structure or generalized schemata which governs behavior" (p. 32).

Behaviorist orientation. Theories in behaviorism, extracted from the learning and psychology fields, have been influencing reading and language arts instruction for many years (Morrison et al., 1999). The behaviorist view of reading regards the activity as a highly mechanical bottom-up process (Gough, 1972).

Influenced by theories from Ivan Pavlov, John B. Watson, and B. F. Skinner, reading theorists including Gough (1972, 1993), LaBerge and Samuels (1974), and Rayner and Pollastek (1989), reading is defined from a language-decoding perspective and believed that English reading means literally the mechanical process of going through materials or text printed or written in the English language (Zainal, 2003). Therefore, reading in this orientation processes two primary features. First, recognizing the individual language units – such as words, sentences, or text – should be the readers' focus (Morrison et al., 1999; Zainal, 2003). Second, the focus is not on the cognitivist process of understanding the text in this orientation (Gough, 1972).

Given this background on a behaviorist orientation, the following were representative excerpts from the teachers' survey responses on the meaning of reading English:

> Example 1: "All reading materials that are written in English language or that relate to the English language in any other languages."

> Example 2: "It means the reading of English articles; the articles may be written by English native speakers or non-native speakers."

> Example 3: "Reading materials printed in English ..."

> Example 4: "English [reading] means much to me. First, improve the learners' reading skills, enlarge the learners' vocabularies."

> Example 5: "It means reading in English which is formal and refined. This kind of reading requires a certain amount of vocabulary. The sentences are complex and a little difficult to understand."

Cognitivist orientation. Three features emerged from analyzing participants' beliefs within the cognitivist orientation. First, the role of the reader's schema and the importance of the reading materials or texts are given equal emphasis within a typical cognitivist reading model (DeFord, 1978; Goodman, 1967). Goodman (1967) stated that "reading is a psychological guessing game. It involves an interaction between thought and language" (p. 2). A reader's comprehension of the desired information is more important than the information itself. That is, processing the information is more important than simply seeking and acquiring the information (Goodman, 1986; Morrison et al., 1999). Advocating the cognitivist view of reading, Smith (1971) and Goodman (1967) criticized the behaviorist view of reading for its overemphasis on decoding the text.

Second, meanings of each language unit are conditioned or defined by the reader's experience and knowledge, which means the reader's comprehension might be different from the author's intention due to his/her different experiences and understandings (Barlett, 1932; Rumelhart, 1977, 1980).

Third, cognitivism is a combination of behaviorism and Gestalt's thinking on proximity, similarity, and traces with their effects on learning as a whole (e.g., Rumelhart, 1977). This kind of combination overlaps and surpasses tenets in behaviorism. While both orientations agree that reading deals with information, the cognitivist orientation focuses on seeking and processing the information in the text. The following excerpts provided evidence of teachers holding dominant cognitivist reading orientations:

> Example 1: "English reading refers to a process; by reading, one can fully understand the material and the author's thought, and during this process, one can learn a lot of things."

> Example 2: "For me, English reading can be divided into intensive and extensive reading. The former requires readers to analyze sentence/text structure, content, and expressions. The latter requires readers to comprehend the content from an overall perspective."

> Example 3: "To comprehend and get information through reading in a specific time slot. To comprehend the referential meaning of the text and also share the reader's own understanding and perspectives."

It should be noted that reading as a skill may fall into both behaviorist and cognitivist orientations, as there is a blur between the two in terms of how the skill is used and developed. If the primary function of the skill is to *seek* and *process* information, then these types of thoughts and beliefs are a design feature for the cognitivist reading orientation (Goodman, 1967, 1986; Smith, 1971). However, if the skill is developed only to help a reader mechanically answer test questions, it shows a behaviorist belief. Examples 4 and 5 below are excerpts from each paradigm, respectively, and Example 6 is a combination of the two. All the excerpts were from the participants' survey responses:

> Example 4: "Reading is the most important skill for English ... to seek and process information in the reading text."

Example 5: "It refers to skimming or scanning for information and appreciation and understanding of the meaning between the lines. It involves speed, depth, and width of reading."

Example 6: "For me, English reading can be divided into two types. The first is reading for testing purposes, that is, how to read to answer questions well. The second is reading for daily use, that is, how to read to enlarge vocabulary and learn."

Constructivist orientation. In terms of the dominant, constructivist reading orientation, teachers' responses in this category also met one or more of three criteria.

First, *meaning* is at the core of the constructivist theory. Mental interactions between readers and writers then become the medium in which readers construct the meaning of the text (Rosenblatt, 1994; Rumelhart, 1980; Stanovich, 1980). Reutzel and Cooter (1996) stated that "readers must integrate an array of information sources from the text and from their background experiences to construct a valid interpretation of the author's message recorded in the text" (p. 49).

Second, readers also construct the meaning of the text through a linguistic cueing system that consists of knowledge from syntax, semantics, and pragmatics. Instead of simply a *bottom-up* (behaviorist) or *top-down* (cognitive) process, reading becomes a holistic and recycled process from the part to the whole and then the whole to the part (Rosenblatt, 1994; Rumelhart, 1980; Stanovich, 1980).

Third, real-life situations play an important role in guiding readers to construct the meaning of the text (Bernhardt, 1986; Coady, 1979; Stanovich, 1980). Excerpt examples from the participants' survey definitions of reading include:

Example 1: "The interaction among the readers, the writer, and the text."

Example 2: "[To] fully understand the author's intention of writing; appreciate the beauty of original works; read as much as possible"

Example 3: "[T]he reader can enjoy the reading itself."

Some teachers' stated beliefs about reading indicated the presence of two reading belief systems – for example, a dual reading orientation between behaviorism and cognitivism. Excerpts to support this kind of presence are as follows:

Example 1: "English reading means a lot to me. It is the best way to improve your comprehensive reading skills, enrich your vocabulary, and board [broaden] your horizon."

Example 2: "English reading is [to] read through a text, process it, and understand its meaning and ideas."

Example 3: "Efficient in reading which might include reading quickly, obtaining necessary information and forming his/her own opinions to agree or not."

The above examples focused not only on reading skills and vocabulary (features of a behaviorist orientation) but also on ways to broaden one's mindset and get a deeper understanding of the text. In this way, they showed the features of both behaviorism and cognitivism. Some teachers held a dual reading orientation between cognitivism and constructivism. For example:

Example 1: "To comprehend and get information through reading in a specific time slot. To comprehend the referential meaning of the text and also share the reader's own understanding and perspectives."

Example 2: "English reading means being informed and touched."

Still other teachers held dual reading orientations, including both behaviorism and constructivism. Excerpts to support this kind of presence were listed as follows:

Example 1: "English reading, for me, means reading extensively and critically in English; it can be novels, practical sciences, etc."

Example 2: "It is a way to obtain information, entertainment or wisdom through visual capability in the language of English."

The multiple theoretical orientation referred to teachers' stated beliefs about reading that indicated the presence of all three reading belief systems (11.1% of teachers fell into this category). Excerpts to support this kind of presence included the following definitions of reading:

Example 1: "Ability to read English works; English works should be at the level of English proficiency; understand the meaning of author & works."

Example 2: "It is a language skill; it is a tool to get information via English; it is a window open to another culture."

Example 3: "To get information about what you need; to get knowledge about vocabulary and cultures."

2.2.2   Feature Analysis of the Teaching Beliefs

Just as the above section detailed qualitative excerpts regarding reading beliefs, the following section provides qualitative survey excerpts with further explanation of the nature of the participants' teaching beliefs.

All of the three theoretical orientations, i.e., behaviorism, cognitivism, and constructivism, were found in survey responses from teachers' stated beliefs about teaching reading. In addition, questions about reading beliefs also indicated specific orientations in teaching beliefs. For example, information on how participants viewed themselves as readers also reflects on their beliefs about teaching reading.

If their teaching beliefs fell into the behaviorist orientation, teachers emphasized measurable and static outcomes. For example, to evaluate whether the students had a sufficient vocabulary and were able to read the words accurately and fluently, teachers typically used read-aloud and decoding methods. Teachers in the behaviorist orientation also emphasized simple and early steps, which they stated would then lead to more complex levels of performance (Ertmer & Newby, 2013). Representative instructional methods under that emphasis include sentence-making practice, pattern drills, etc. (Zainal, 2003).

Another stated preference of teachers with behaviorist beliefs is to examine and evaluate students from their learning or review of previous lectures, for example, dictations of words learned in the previous text. Table 5 lists sample excerpts from the teachers' written beliefs indicating the different methods in the behaviorist orientation.

Teachers who held beliefs in the cognitivist orientation generally emphasized reader comprehension and understanding. A reader's *comprehension* of the information rather than the *information* itself is more important (Goodman, 1986; Morrison et al., 1999). For example, a cognitivist teacher may regularly check students' understanding of a certain word or phrase. Also, teachers in a cognitivist orientation acknowledge the importance of experience and background knowledge and prefer to teach background information or cultural background knowledge about the reading text to the students (Bernhardt, 1986; Coady, 1979; Stanovich, 1980).

TABLE 5   Sample excerpts from stated teaching beliefs with behaviorist emphases

Behaviorist emphases	Sample excerpts/keywords in stated beliefs
Decoding system	Grasp the main points and keywords
	Use of transitional words
	Ensure the amount of the vocabulary as input
Part to whole	Deal with some language notes by making sentences
(bottom-up process)	Find the transitive words in what they read
	Enlarge the amount of reading materials
	Use the given words to make sentences
Preassessment/repetition	Dictation
(response-stimulus)	Read aloud
	Fluent reading

TABLE 6   Sample excerpts from stated teaching beliefs with cognitivist emphases

Cognitivist emphases	Sample excerpts/keywords in stated beliefs
Active thinking	Predict the meaning of vocabulary you meet
(comprehension)	Refer to what you have learned
	Reading strategies that help readers to process the information
	Understand the sentence and the words
Whole to part	Read the text as a whole to infer the word meaning
(top-down process)	Notice the transition of each paragraph
	Summarize the general idea for a better understanding
Prior knowledge	Background knowledge
(schemata)	Cultural background
	Text learned before
	Guiding questions

In addition, as the cognitivist orientation focuses on the seeking and processing of the information read in the text, teachers in this paradigm tend to teach students reading strategies that help them to process the information (Morrison et al., 1999). The excerpts from survey responses in Table 6 provide examples of teachers holding a dominant, cognitivist teaching orientation.

Teachers' responses indicating teaching beliefs in the constructivist orientation included a couple of key characteristics. First, because the mental interaction between readers and writers is considered the process through which readers construct the meaning of the text, teachers prefer to guide the student readers to construct their own personal meaning (Goodman, 1967; Smith, 1971). In constructivism, teachers emphasize their role as guides or facilitators instead of instructors (Morrison et al., 1999; Zainal, 2003). Also, since real-life situations and affective factors play an important role in guiding the readers to construct the meaning, teachers tend to teach the student readers how to construct an understanding of the text through their past experiences in the real world (Morrison et al., 1999; Zainal, 2003). Table 7 lists sample excerpts from the teachers' stated beliefs indicating the different methods they used within the constructivist orientation.

In this section, findings indicated that complexity was the primary feature of the belief system. Specifically, three major theoretical orientations (behaviorism, cognitivism, and constructivism) were matrixed with three types of belief systems, or subbeliefs (dominant, dual, and multiple). This multilayered matrix made the belief system complex. Under the complex matrix, quantitative findings of the study further indicated that there were more complex relationships among beliefs within a specific theoretical orientation and across different orientations. Discussion on only one research question may not provide a holistic picture of the characteristics of the belief system. Therefore, some of these complex relationships within the belief system were explained through discussions on a second research question as well.

In this study, instead of holding a single, unique orientation, most teachers surveyed indicated multiple and diverse reading and teaching orientations. Multiple orientations made the belief system complex. Quantitative findings

TABLE 7   Sample excerpts from stated teaching beliefs with constructivist emphases

Constructivist emphases	Sample excerpts/keywords in stated beliefs
Interaction with writers	Guess the real meaning of the authors
Context	Infer the meaning from the context
Real-world situations	Associate with what s/he has already experienced in reality
	Suppose a scenario that s/he experienced
Affective factors	Foster students' interest
	Motivate students to read

indicated that no matter in reading beliefs or reading teaching beliefs, any orientation was different from the others in its percentage. There was no even distribution among the three reading belief systems or theoretical orientations. For example, teachers with a dominant, constructivist reading orientation accounted for only 3.9%, whereas teachers holding a dominant, behaviorist reading orientation (the most common in the study) accounted for only 18.1%.

Another example is that teachers with a dual reading belief system accounted for 38.8% of the whole sample, whereas teachers holding a multiple reading belief system accounted for only 11.1%. In addition to the complex coexistence of different theoretical orientations, the findings of the study indicated that relationships among different beliefs were nonlinear and unpredictable. Specifically, statistical percentages of a certain belief system did not necessarily indicate similar percentages of the belief system in teaching and vice versa. For example, the largest percentage in reading beliefs was the dual belief system (38.8%), whereas the largest percentage in reading teacing beliefs was the single, behaviorist belief system (37.8%).

The nonlinear, unpredictable relationship then made the participants' teacher belief systems even more complex. This finding was similar to study findings regarding teachers' stated beliefs about teaching reading (Pajares, 1992; Phipps & Borg, 2009; Skott, 2001). By joining the existing literature, I also provided hypothetical, empirical, and theoretical explanations for this complex phenomenon.

Basturkmen (2012) offered one hypothetical explanation for the diversity of belief systems held among teachers: their different educational and professional backgrounds and/or teaching experiences. She stated that "more experienced teachers are likely to have more experientially informed beliefs than relative novices, and principles or beliefs informed by teaching experiences might be expected to correspond clearly with teaching practices" (Basturkmen, 2012). This idea was not mirrored in the current study, as the emerging young teachers, Y, and D in Case Study 1, had the most consistency in their beliefs of everyone in the group.

Senior (2006) offered another hypothesis. After investigating teachers' decision-making abilities in their classrooms, Senior (2006) hypothesized that teachers appeared to hold different/contradictory belief systems because their abilities to articulate or state their beliefs about reading varied from person to person. In some ways, findings in this study confirmed this hypothesis. Some Chinese EFL teachers spoke more than others in describing or explaining what they believed to be "good" reading or readers. For example, Y's stated responses to the survey questions contained richer information on how he thought about reading and teaching reading. Similar to Y, L stated her beliefs about reading and reading instruction in more detail than the other teachers in the survey. Both relied on examples, hypothetical teaching practices, and philosophical statements to make their points clear.

Some studies have offered one hypothesis from the perspective of teacher reflection. For example, Gatbonton (2008) found that novice or inexperienced teachers were less likely to reflect on their instructions, as they might spend more time planning or designing lesson plans. In addition, Farrell (1999) hypothesized that the varied beliefs about reading among different teachers might also be related to the frequency or quality of the teachers' reflections. While the study was not able to explore how much reflection each teacher had made through survey data and classroom observations, it will present why reflection is important in solving the tensions between beliefs and practices in the last section of the chapter.

Moving beyond the hypotheses, scholars proposed different theories to explain the dynamic, unpredictable nature of belief systems. For example, the theory of action (e.g., Li, 2013) and chaos theory (e.g., Zheng, 2013b) are both attempts to account for why a belief system is dynamic and complex. For example, Li (2013), from the theory-of-action perspective, found that "no strict one-to-one correspondence" but a complex relationship existed between beliefs and practices (p. 175). The theory-of-action perspective links humans' thoughts with their actions, and indicates that humans' behaviors respond to context. Contextual influence is thus key to explaining the complex relationships found in both that and the current research.

Zheng (2013a), from the chaos theory perspective, used a case study in a Chinese secondary school to explore features of teacher belief systems and how different types of beliefs interacted to inform teacher practice. The chaos theory is a great fit to study systems, teachers' belief systems included, that are "produced by a set of components that interact in particular ways to produce some overall state or form at a particular point in time" (Larsen-Freeman & Cameron, 2008, p. 26). Zheng's study confirmed the complex, nonlinear features of the belief system and suggested an eclectic approach, including ideas from several perspectives, as a way to ease the tensions between teachers' beliefs and practices. Findings of the present study, particularly the diversity in practices, held with that idea.

A final finding in this study regarding teacher's stated beliefs was that while the largest group of teachers held a behaviorist belief, the percentage of teachers holding a dominant constructivist orientation was larger than that of the teachers holding the dominant cognitivist orientation. Previous studies (e.g., Johnson, 1992; Kırkgöz, 2008) found that the temporary innovations in language teaching affect teachers as they form their dominant beliefs. For example, Johnson (1992) found that the dominance of the function-based theoretical orientation at the time when she was doing the research represented the overwhelming popularity of the approach among ESL teachers in her study. The recent push to implement constructivist practices in education reform may account for part of that philosophical dominance.

3   Conceptualization of the Dynamics and Agents in the Belief System

Through the quantitative data and the qualitative excerpts provided above, I gradually summarized and reported the general characteristics of the belief system, including the complexity of the belief system and the nonlinearity and unpredictability of the subsystems. Through the process of describing, reporting, and summarizing the data, I found it necessary to conceptualize the findings and draw theoretical implications at the end of this chapter.

Considerable dynamics or agents are included in the belief system of reading (see Figure 3). These dynamics or agents are the unit of analysis in the study, metaphorically compared to a cell in an organism. As the study particularly focuses on reading and reading orientations, each dynamic and agent may include a specific piece of reading or reading teaching beliefs or a specific theoretical orientation guiding the belief or the actual practice. These dynamics and agents are represented by different shapes, sizes, and colors. Specifically, each shape represents a certain theoretical orientation to reading which serves as a certain dynamic or agent: a diamond stands for a behaviorist orientation, an oval for a cognitivist orientation, and a star for a constructivist orientation.

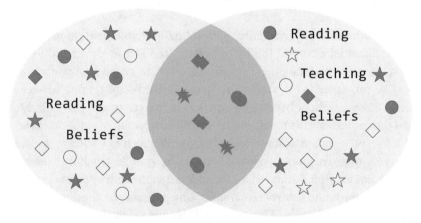

FIGURE 3   Dynamics and agents in the belief system

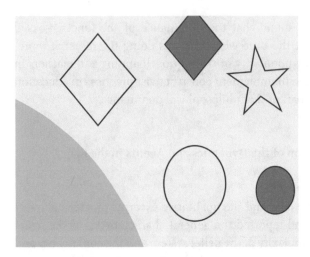

FIGURE 4
Representations of reading
orientations and beliefs

Each size represents the scope and power of a dynamic or agent. For example, a big diamond represents a core, behaviorist orientation, and a small diamond represents a peripheral, behaviorist orientation. Similarly, a big oval represents a core, cognitivist orientation, and a small oval represents a peripheral, cognitivist orientation; a big star represents a core, constructivist orientation and a small star represents a peripheral, constructivist orientation. All the different sizes of dynamics and agents coexist and interact in the holistic system (see Figure 4).

The colored or uncolored dynamics or agents indicate their implicitness or explicitness. Specifically, a colored dynamic or agent represents an explicit belief or orientation in guiding the belief and practice; a blank or uncolored dynamic or agent stands for an implicit belief or orientation. For example, a colored diamond represents a certain explicit, behaviorist orientation or belief.

3.1   *Dynamics in Different Shapes: How Do Different Orientations Work?*

In the conceptual nexus of the belief system (see Figure 5), three different reading orientations, including behaviorism, cognitivism, and constructivism, coexist. As presented in the previous chapters, DeFord's (1985) TORP was referenced to assess teachers' beliefs and practices in this study, and particularly to design the coding rubric for data analysis. This survey consists of 28 items and used a five-point Likert scale to assess teachers' agreement with statements about reading instruction. It aims to investigate three instructional orientations: (1) phonics, which emphasizes sound-letter units, with a gradual progression toward words and sentences, (2) skills, which focuses on the development of sight words; and (3) whole language, which aims to get children immersed

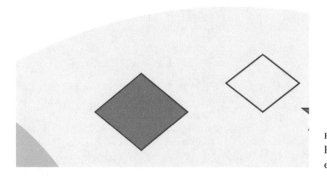

FIGURE 5
Representations of different reading orientations

in meaningful and quality literature and working them down toward smaller
language units. Based on the categories, I further listed behaviorism, cognitivism, and constructivism as the three reading orientations for the current study.
They are presented in the form of three different shapes, including diamond,
oval, and star. A matrix of the three shapes and orientations is presented in
Figure 5.

3.2   *Dynamics in Different Sizes: How Do Core vs. Peripheral Beliefs Work?*

Also, in the conceptual nexus of a belief system (see Figure 6), different sizes
of the dynamics or agents indicate whether they are core or peripheral orientations. In a multiple theoretical orientation to reading system, core and
peripheral beliefs coexist. A core belief was similar to a dominant belief; it outperformed peripheral beliefs in percentage and frequency in the belief system.
This finding was in accordance with Borg's (2003, 2006, 2009) work on teacher
cognition and practice.

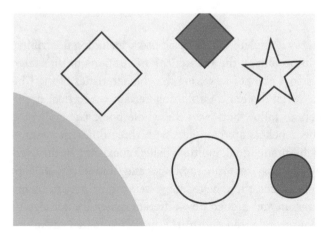

FIGURE 6
Representations of
core vs. peripheral
beliefs

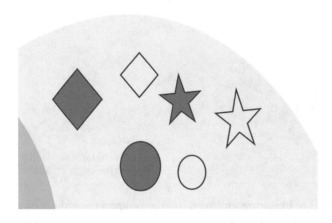

FIGURE 7
Representations of
implicit vs. explicit
beliefs

3.3   *Dynamics in Different Colors: How Do Implicit vs. Explicit Beliefs Work?*

Last but not least, in the conceptual nexus of the belief system (see Figure 7), different colors of the dynamics or agents indicate whether they are explicit or implicit orientations. Based on Pajares (1992), scholars further divided teachers' beliefs into explicit and implicit ones. Espoused or explicit beliefs are what a person can readily articulate (Johnson, 1992), and implicit beliefs are held unconsciously and inferred from actions (Argyris & Schön, 1974; Breen et al., 2001). However, Borg (2011) stated that there is some disagreement on conscious vs. unconscious beliefs, with some people regarding consciousness as an inherent attribute of beliefs, and the others holding that beliefs can be either conscious or unconscious.

4   Conclusion

In this chapter, I primarily completed three basic tasks, including describing, summarizing, and conceptualizing the theoretical orientations in the stated belief system. By doing so, I aim at presenting the characteristics of the Chinese reading teachers' belief system and offering certain theoretical implications for the chapters to follow and even the whole book. Generally, the Chinese reading teachers' beliefs are complex, with three different types of subsystems, including dominant, dual, multiple beliefs coexisting in the overall system. However, these subsystems are nonlinear and unpredictable. With those findings, I conceptualized these belief subsystems to be dynamics and agents in the overall system and argued how different dynamics and agents might work in their power and strength. (In the next chapter, I will further explore the interactive nature of the stated beliefs of reading and the stated beliefs of teaching reading among the participating teachers.)

Acknowledgment

Part of this chapter was published as Gao, Y., & Bintz, W. P. (2019). An exploratory study on Chinese EFL teachers' beliefs about reading and teaching reading. *The Journal of Asia TEFL, 16*(2), 576–590. While adaptation has been thoroughly made for the current chapter, credits are still acknowledged for my publication and the journal.

References

Argyris, C., & Schön, D. A. (1974). *Theory in practice: Increasing professional effectiveness.* Jossey-Bass.

Bartlett, F. C. (1932). *Remembering.* Cambridge University Press.

Basturkmen, H. (2012). Review of research into the correspondence between language teachers' stated beliefs and practices. *System, 40*(2), 282–295. https://doi.org/10.1016/j.system.2012.05.001

Bernhardt, E. (1986). Cognitivist processes in L2: An examination of reading behaviors. In J. Lantolf & L. Labarca (Eds.), *Research in second language learning: Focus on the classroom* (pp. 35–51). Ablex.

Borg, S. (2003). Teacher cognition in language teaching: A review of research into what language teachers think, know, believe and do. *Language Teaching, 36*(2), 81–109.

Borg, S. (2006). *Teacher cognition and language education: Research and practice.* Continuum.

Borg, S. (2009). English language teachers' conceptions of research. *Applied Linguistics, 30*(3), 355–388.

Borg, S. (2011). The impact of in-service education on language teachers' beliefs. *System, 39*(3), 370–380.

Breen, M. P., Hird, B., Milton, M., Oliver, R., & Thwaite. A. (2011). Making sense of language teaching: Teachers' principles and classroom practices. *Applied Linguistics, 22*(4), 470–501.

Coady, J. (1979). A psycholinguistic model of the ESL reader. In R. Mackay, B. Barkman, & R. R. Jordan (Eds.), *Reading in a second language* (pp. 5–12). Newbury House.

Cortazzi, M., & Jin, L. X. (1996). Cultures of learning: Language classrooms in China. In H. Coleman (Ed.), *Society and the language classroom* (pp. 169–206). Cambridge University Press.

Creswell, J. W. (2012). *Qualitative inquiry and research design: Choosing among five traditions* (3rd ed.). Sage.

DeFord, D. (1978). *A validation study of an instrument to determine teachers' theoretical orientation to reading instruction* [PhD dissertation]. Indiana University.

DeFord, D. (1985). Validating the construct of theoretical orientation in reading instruction. *Reading Research Quarterly, 20*(3), 351–367.

Ertmer, P. A., & Newby, T. J. (2013). Behaviorism, cognitivism, constructivism: Comparing critical features from an instructional design perspective. *Performance Improvement Quarterly, 26*(2), 43–71.

Farrell, T. S. C. (1999). The reflective assignment: Unlocking pre-service English teachers' beliefs on grammar teaching. *RELC Journal, 30*(2), 1–17.

Gao, Y. (2013). Incorporating sociocultural theory into second language (L2) reading instruction: A unit plan for EFL learners. *US-China Foreign Languages, 11*(11), 859–869.

Gao, Y., & Bintz, W. P. (2019). An exploratory study on Chinese EFL teachers' beliefs about reading and teaching reading. *The Journal of Asia TEFL, 16*(2), 576–590.

Gatbonton, E. (2008). Looking beyond teachers' classroom behavior: Novice and experienced ESL teachers' pedagogical knowledge. *Language Teaching Research, 12*(2), 161–182.

Goodman, K. (1967). Reading: A psycholinguistic guessing game. *Journal of the Reading Specialist, 6*(4), 126–135.

Goodman, K. (1986). *What's whole in whole language?* Heinemann Educational Books.

Gough, P. B. (1972). Theoretical models and processes of reading. In J. F. Kavanagh & I. G. Mattingly (Eds.), *Language by ear and by eye* (pp. 661–685). MIT Press.

Gough, P. B. (1993). The beginning of decoding. *Reading and Writing: An Interdisciplinary Journal, 5*(2), 181–192.

Gutierrez Almarza, G. (1996). Student foreign language teacher's knowledge growth. In D. Freeman & J. C. Richards (Eds.), *Teacher learning in language teaching* (pp. 50–78). Cambridge University Press.

Harste, J. C., & Burke, C. L. (1977). A new hypothesis for reading teacher research: Both the teaching and learning of reading are theoretically based. In P. D. Pearson (Ed.), *Reading: Theory, research and practice* (pp. 32–40). National Reading Conference.

Hu, G. W. (2002). English language teaching in the People's Republic of China. In R. E. Silver, G. W. Hu, & M. Iino (Eds.), *English language education in China, Japan, and Singapore* (pp. 1–77). National Institute of Education.

Johnson, K. E. (1992). The relationship between teachers' beliefs and practices during literacy instruction for non-native speakers of English. *Journal of Reading Behavior, 24*(1), 83–108.

Kırkgöz, Y. (2008). A case study of teachers' implementation of curriculum innovation in English language teaching in Turkish primary education. *Teaching and Teacher Education, 24*(7), 1859–1875.

LaBerge, D., & Samuels, S. (1974). Toward a theory of automatic information processing in reading. *Cognitivist Psychology, 6*(2), 293–323.

Larsen-Freeman, D., & Cameron, L. (2008). Research methodology on language development from a complex systems perspective. *The Modern Language Journal, 92*(2), 200–213.

Li, L. (2013). The complexity of language teachers' beliefs and practice: One EFL teacher's theories. *The Language Learning Journal, 41*(2), 175–191. https://doi.org/10.1080/09571736.2013.790132

Merriam, S. (1998). *Qualitative research and case study applications in education.* Jossey-Bass.

Morrison, T. G., Wilcox, B., Madrigal, J. L., Roberts, S., & Hintze, E. (1999). Teachers' theoretical orientations toward reading and pupil control ideology: A national survey. *Reading Research and Instruction, 38*(4), 333–350.

Ng, C., & Tang, E. (1997). Teachers' needs in the process of EFL reform in China – A report from Shanghai. *Perspectives: Working Papers, 9*(1), 63–85.

Pajares, M. F. (1992). Teachers' beliefs and educational research: Cleaning up a messy construct. *Review of Educational Research, 62*(3), 307–332.

Peterson, B. E., & Williams, S. R. (1998). Mentoring beginning teachers. *Mathematics Teacher, 91*(8), 730–734.

Phipps, S., & Borg, S. (2009). Exploring tensions between teachers' grammar teaching beliefs and practices. *System, 37*(3), 380–390.

Rayner, K., & Pollatsek, A. (1989). *The psychology of reading.* Prentice Hall.

Reutzel, D., & Cooter, R. B. (1996). *Teaching children to read: From basals to books* (2nd ed.). Merrill/Prentice Hall.

Rosenblatt, L. M. (1994). The transactional theory of reading and writing. In R. B. Ruddell, M. R. Ruddell, & H. Singer (Eds.), *Theoretical models and processes of reading* (4th ed., pp. 1057–1092). International Reading Association.

Rumelhart, D. E. (1977). Understanding and summarizing brief stories. In D. Laberge & S. J. Samuels (Eds.), *Basic processes in reading* (pp. 265–303). Erlbaum.

Rumelhart, D. E. (1980). Schemata: The building blocks of cognition. In R. J. Spiro, B. C. Bruce, & W. F. Brewer (Eds.), *Theoretical issues in reading comprehension* (pp. 33–58). Erlbaum.

Senior, R. (2006). *The experience of language teaching.* Cambridge University Press.

Skott, J. (2001). The emerging practices of a novice teacher: The roles of his school mathematics images. *Journal of Mathematics Teacher Education, 4*(1), 3–28.

Smith, F. (1971). *Understanding reading.* Holt, Rinehart & Winston.

Stanovich, K. E. (1980). Toward an interactive-compensatory model of individual differences in the development of reading fluency. *Reading Research Quarterly, 16*(1), 32–71.

Vygotsky, L. S. (1978). *Mind in society: The development of higher psychological processes.* Harvard University Press.

Yin, R. K. (2003). *Case study research: Design and methods.* Sage.

Zainal, Z. (2003). Critical review of reading model and theories in first and second language. *Human Journal/Jurnal Kemanusiaan, 1*(2), 104–124.

Zheng, H. (2013a). The dynamic interactive relationship between Chinese secondary school EFL teachers' beliefs and practice. *The Language Learning Journal, 41*(2), 192–204. https://doi.org/10.1080/09571736.2013.790133

Zheng, H. (2013b). Teachers' beliefs and practices: A dynamic and complex relationship. *Asia-Pacific Journal of Teacher Education, 41*(3), 331–343. https://doi.org/10.1080/1359866X.2013.809051

Exploring Interaction between Reading Beliefs and Reading Teaching Beliefs in Dominant Orientations

1   Introduction

I presented quantitative data and qualitative excerpts to describe the general characteristics of Chinese EFL teachers' reading beliefs and reading teaching beliefs in the previous chapter. In this chapter, I will continue exploring the relationship between the two constructs (reading beliefs vs. reading teaching beliefs) through both quantitative, statistical results and qualitative, interpretivist analysis. In my original draft, I was thinking about revealing the consistency or inconsistency between the two constructs. However, further consideration made me realize the so-called (in)consistency may be too vague to be described. Therefore, I switched over to explore the interaction between the two constructs and attempted to answer these questions: What is the relationship between the reading beliefs and reading teaching beliefs? Are the reading beliefs consistently revealed through the reading teaching beliefs?

It is challenging to propose a specific research question, as researchers from two different camps, the quantitative and the qualitative, may pay attention to the wording such as "what" and "how" and assert their own preeminence. However, the pragmatic nature of employing a mixed-method design is indeed beneficial in that using mixed data can complement findings from the two solitary camps. Therefore, I would rather explain the *aim* of the second research question rather than simply posit it, causing debates or raising concerns in the two camps. I attempt to explore *the relationship and interaction* between the two constructs.

2   Analyses of Reading Beliefs vs. Teaching Beliefs in the Dominant Orientations

While the question is presented in a way more likely to be suitable for a qualitative answer, I also used some statistical analyses to support the argument. These statistical analyses serve to generate a general rather than a specific picture of the consistency between the two constructs. With that general picture, specific analyses or descriptions would be provided to explore the interaction between the two constructs. Therefore, I assume that any consistency between reading beliefs and reading teaching beliefs would indicate a certain interaction between the reading beliefs and the teaching beliefs. At the same time, any inconsistency would indicate little interaction between the two constructs. To examine the (in)consistency, I used a crosstab and reported the Cohen's kappa and chi-square statistics. It is worth mentioning that only analyses of the three dominant orientations were included in the study, hoping that the way analyzed and used may provide future research with some insights to extend the line of inquiry, particularly for exploring tensions among the dual and multiple orientations. Analyses of these beliefs and practices also required a detailed, systemic coding rubric, which will be presented in the following section.

2.1   *Guideline and Rubric for the Coding*

Based on Kinzer (1988), Johnson (1992) used a multidimensional TESL theoretical orientation protocol to conduct a study in the same field. The protocol also included two triads of categories in both reading and reading teaching beliefs. The categories are *skill-based*, *rule-based*, and *function-based*, which resemble Kinzer's triads. While the terms representing categories are different, they actually indicate the same theoretical orientations (see Table 8). It should be mentioned that the term *skill-based*, while appearing twice in different orientations, does have different meanings. For Johnson (1992), the term indicates reading is a separate language skill compared with writing, listening, and speaking. In a behaviorist sense, the term means language learners use their reading skills to recognize words or textual patterns. However, the term in the cognitivist domain indicates readers use reading as a skill to comprehend or process information in the text.

Categorical variables. Categorical variables, as the name implies, are defined as variables that consist of a set of categories (Creswell, 2009). Generally, there are three major types of categorical variables: nominal, ordinal, and interval. *Nominal* variables have categories with no natural order to them, which are different from *ordinal* variables, which occur in a natural order. *Interval* variables

TABLE 8   Categorical variable sets in the previous studies

	Behaviorism	Cognitivism	Constructivism
DeFord (1978)	Phonics	Skill-based	Whole language
Kinzer (1988)	Text-based	Reader-based	Interactive
Johnson (1992)	Skill-based	Rule-based	Function-based

TABLE 9   Categorical variable sets in the study

	Reading survey	Teaching survey	Adapted TORP
Variable set 1	Text-based – 1	Rote teaching-based – 1	Behaviorism – 1
Variable set 2	Meaning-based – 2	Comprehension-based – 2	Cognitivism – 2
Variable set 3	Function-based – 3	Interactive – 3	Constructivism – 3

are created from intervals on a continuous scale. Based on the previous studies, the present study uses sets of the nominal type of categorical variable (see Table 9).

In total, nine categorical nominal variables that are within three sets were defined in this study. Set 1 consists of three variables on teachers' beliefs of English reading models: text-based, comprehension-based, and interactive approaches. Set 2 consists of three variables on teachers' beliefs of English reading teaching approaches: rote teaching-based, comprehension-based, and interactive approaches. Set 3 consists of three categorical variables representing teachers' theoretical orientations revealed in the adapted TORP: behaviorism, cognitivism, and constructivism. The researcher named each variable in each set with a number for the sake of quantitative analysis. For example, the phonics model in Set 1 is marked as 1, comprehension-based teaching is marked as 2 in Set 2, and constructivism theory is marked as 3 in Set 3.

2.2   Analysis of Reading Beliefs vs. Teaching Beliefs in the Behaviorist Orientation

Behaviorism (Watson, 1913), also termed behavioral psychology, is a theory of learning based on the idea that all behaviors are acquired through conditioning (Skinner, 1938). As one of the educational paradigms, behaviorism has exerted a great influence on all aspects of education and language learning for decades (e.g., Harasim, 2017). In the view of a reading behaviorist (e.g., Gough, 1972; Rayner & Pollastek, 1989), reading as a source of learning takes place when it is separated into smaller bits. Reading instruction focuses on conditioning the reader's behavior (Morrison et al., 1999). Teaching methods involve repetition and association, which are highly mechanical (Shuman, 1986). Behaviorist reading teachers believe that a certain behavioral pattern should be repeated until it becomes automatic. Therefore, methods including reading aloud, dictation, and direct/rote instruction are typically used in reading class (Morrison et al., 1999; Zainal, 2003). These behaviorist beliefs about reading and reading instruction were also revealed in the current study. However, the statistical

TABLE 10   Cross tabulation of behaviorism reading/teaching orientations

			T1		
			0	1	Total
R1	0	Count	27	60	87
		% within R1	31.0%	69.0%	100.0%
	1	Count	75	226	301
		% within R1	24.9%	75.1%	100.0%
Total		Count	102	286	388
		% within R1	26.3%	73.7%	100.0%

Notes: Chi(df) = 1.303(1), p = .254; kappa = .058
      R1 = behaviorist reading beliefs; T1 = behaviorist teaching beliefs

results did not indicate an association between the reading beliefs and the teaching beliefs (see Table 10).

Table 10 shows that 75.1% of the teachers who held reading beliefs in the behaviorist orientation consistently applied that orientation to their teaching beliefs. However, 69.0% of the teachers who did not hold such an orientation in their reading beliefs were also able to express the behaviorist orientation in their teaching beliefs. There were no significant differences. That is, whether teachers held the behaviorist reading beliefs did not affect whether they held behaviorist teaching beliefs. Likewise, 31.0% of the teachers had neither behaviorist reading beliefs nor behaviorist teaching beliefs. However, 24.9% of those teachers without the behaviorist orientation in their teaching beliefs showed the behaviorist orientation in their reading beliefs. That is, whether or not teachers held behaviorist teaching beliefs was not associated with their behaviorist reading beliefs (see Table 10).

To assess the difference in frequencies in reading beliefs versus teaching beliefs, I used a chi-square analysis, which accounted for the different count data in each category, and examined the distribution across the contingency table in Table 10. I found that the differences were not independent of chance ($\chi2(df = 1) = 1.303$, $p = .254$). In other words, there was no significant difference in frequencies of behaviorist teaching beliefs between teachers who held behaviorist reading beliefs and those who did not hold behaviorist reading beliefs. Therefore, reading beliefs and teaching beliefs in the behaviorist orientation were not associated but independent of each other.

To examine the consistency between reading beliefs and teaching beliefs in the behaviorist orientation, I also used Cohen's kappa, which showed the proportion of agreement over and above chance agreement. In the study, the kappa coefficient indicated how much the proportion of consistency (beyond the chance agreement) would be between reading beliefs and teaching beliefs in a specific theoretical orientation. Cohen's kappa (κ) can range from minus 1 to plus 1, and the current research showed that Cohen's kappa (κ) was .058. Based on the guidelines from Altman (1999) and adapted from Landis and Koch (1977), a kappa (κ) of .058 represents a slight strength of agreement. Therefore, reading beliefs and teaching beliefs, in a behaviorist orientation, were slightly consistent.

2.3   Analysis of Reading Beliefs vs. Teaching Beliefs in the Cognitivist Orientation

Different from a behaviorist, a cognitivist believes that learning is a change in individuals' mental structures, which then renders changes in behavior (Ertmer & Newby, 2013). Ormrod (2008) stated:

> Many cognitive theories focus on how people think about (i.e., *process*) the information they receive from the environment, how they perceive the stimuli around them, how they "put" what they've perceived into their *memories*, how they "find" what they've learned when they need to use it, and so on. ... [This is] collectively known as "*information processing theory.*" (p. 163)

To be more specific, the thought processes behind behavior is more important for a person's learning (Goodman, 1967). With reference to reading and reading instruction, reading comprehension and skills/strategies rather than reading text or language units are what readers and reading teachers are most concerned with (Ertmer & Newby, 2013; Morrison et al., 1999; Zainal, 2003).

In this study, statistical results failed to support consistency between teachers' cognitivist reading beliefs and their cognitivist teaching beliefs (see Table 11). To assess the difference in frequencies in reading beliefs vs. teaching beliefs in the cognitivist orientation, I used a chi-square analysis, which accounted for the different count data in each category, and examined the distribution across the contingency table in Table 11.

I found that the differences were not independent from chance ($\chi 2(df = 1) = 1.387, p = .239$). In other words, there was no significant difference in frequencies of cognitivist teaching beliefs between teachers who held cognitivist reading beliefs and those who did not hold cognitivist reading beliefs. To be more

TABLE 11   Cross tabulation of cognitivism reading/teaching orientations

			T2		
			o	1	Total
R2	o	Count	121	64	185
		% within R2	65.4%	34.6%	100.0%
	1	Count	121	82	203
		% within R2	59.6%	40.4%	100.0%
Total		Count	242	146	388
		% within R2	62.4%	37.6%	100.0%

Notes: Chi(df) = 1.387(1), p = .239; kappa = .057
       R2 = cognitivist reading beliefs; T2 = cognitivist teaching beliefs

specific, while the percentage of teachers who held cognitivist reading beliefs and then applied them to their teaching beliefs was 40.4%, the percentage of teachers who did not hold cognitivist reading beliefs but then showed the cognitivist orientation in their teaching beliefs was 34.6%. There was only a slight (not a significant) difference. Therefore, reading beliefs and teaching beliefs in the cognitivist orientation were not related.

The result can also be explained through the kappa coefficient. Cohen's kappa (κ) was only .057, which represented a slight strength of agreement. In other words, reading beliefs and teaching beliefs, in a cognitivist orientation, were slightly consistent.

2.4   *Analysis of Reading Beliefs vs. Teaching Beliefs in the Constructivist Orientation*

A constructivist teacher and a constructivist classroom show marked differences from a behaviorist or cognitivist instructor or classroom. A constructivist teacher prefers to incorporate ongoing experiences into student learning by focusing on the negotiation and construction of meaning among small groups and individuals (Lantolf, 2000). When it comes to reading and reading instruction, teachers believe that reading is about discussing and communicating with authors of the text and that instruction should focus on how to encourage students to read and learn by peer discussion (Cambria & Guthrie, 2010). Reading should not be only about language units but also about the appreciation of what you read (Wilson & Yang, 2007).

TABLE 12   Cross tabulation of constructivism reading/teaching orientations

			T3		
			0	1	Total
R3	0	Count	114	98	212
		% within R3	53.8%	46.2%	100.0%
	1	Count	72	104	176
		% within R3	40.9%	59.1%	100.0%
Total		Count	186	202	388
		% within R3	47.9%	52.1%	100.0%

Notes: Chi(df) = 6.377(1), p = .012; kappa = .127
    R3 = constructivist reading beliefs; T3 = constructivist teaching beliefs

In the study, the research showed a slight strength of agreement (κ = 0.127). In other words, reading beliefs and teaching beliefs, in a constructivist orientation, were slightly consistent (see Table 12). However, the chi-square analysis, which accounted for the different count data in each category and examined the distribution across the contingency table in Table 12, showed that the differences were independent of chance ($\chi 2(df = 1)$ = 6.377, p = .012).

In other words, there were significant differences in frequencies of constructivist teaching beliefs between teachers who held constructivist reading beliefs and those who did not hold constructivist reading beliefs. To be more specific, the percentage of teachers who held constructivist reading beliefs and then applied them to their teaching beliefs was 59.1%, whereas the percentage of teachers who did not hold constructivist reading beliefs but then showed the constructivist orientation in their teaching beliefs was 46.2%. There was a statistically significant difference in terms of the percentages, which means teachers in the study who held constructivist reading beliefs could apply the constructivist orientation to their teaching beliefs.

3   Possible Explanations for the Interaction

The chapter investigated whether Chinese EFL teachers' stated beliefs about English reading were consistently indicated in their stated beliefs about teaching reading. On the one hand, quantitative findings from this study indicated that there was a statistically significant association between reading beliefs and teaching beliefs only in the constructivist orientation ($p < .05$). However, the association was not statistically strong ($\phi = .060$, $p < .05$). On the other hand, a statistical association between reading beliefs and teaching beliefs was found in neither behaviorist nor cognitivist orientations. The inconsistent, nonlinear relationships between reading beliefs and reading teaching beliefs made the belief system even more complex.

One reasonable explanation for the consistency between reading beliefs and teaching beliefs in one orientation is that the constructivist theoretical orientation is the most updated theoretical orientation of the three; that is, it has been the subject of the most frequent and current research. Through comparing critical features of the three theoretical orientations, Ertmer and Newby (2013) mapped out how theoretical orientation developed from behaviorism (around 1950) to cognitivism (in the late 1950s), and then to constructivism (in the 1990s). Compared to behaviorism and cognitivism, constructivism is a relatively newer and fresher theoretical orientation and focuses more on how learners construct meaning through their own experiences. As beneficiaries of the most advanced orientation, teachers who read about constructivism or were trained in it experienced an improved engagement with the teaching process. This encounter with constructivism empowers teachers to try new teaching methods derived from that theoretical orientation. Some teacher training programs even advocated for methodological innovation by implementing the updated orientation into practice in their own classes.

Previous studies (e.g., Johnson, 1992; Kırkgöz, 2008) found that temporary innovations in language teaching affect teachers' formations of dominant beliefs. Temporary innovation refers to the methodological innovation in reading instruction derived from an emerging theory at a specific time. For example, when constructivist theory emerged, new instructional methods were developed at the same time, including communicative language learning, task-based learning, and cooperative language learning. Also, some approaches that had been developed following behaviorist and cognitivist orientations may also be redefined in a constructivist way. As mentioned earlier in the study, teachers who used the same instructional approach may have different theoretical orientations. It depends on how teachers would like to use the approach and what kinds of guiding principles are behind the approach. For example, a task-based learning approach can be either behaviorist or constructivist. In this study, if a teacher gave a student a task to repeat reading a certain text as a way to improve his/her reading fluency, he/she has used a behaviorist approach. However, if a teacher gave a student a task to role-play a story by showing how he/she understands the text, he/she has used a constructivist approach. No matter whether it was a newly developed approach or a redefined approach, teachers worked to align their beliefs with their practices in a period of temporary innovation.

Another reasonable explanation for the consistency between reading beliefs and teaching beliefs in teachers with the constructivist view is that those teachers favored and truly believed in the constructivist theoretical orientation. Almarza (1996) found that student teachers at the University of London were taught a specific teaching method during their practicum. However, unless they truly believed in the method, they would not stick to it for long. In other words, only when teachers truly believed in a method would they keep using it. Almarza's findings provide insight into explaining why teachers in the current study exhibited consistent reading beliefs and teaching beliefs in the constructivist theoretical orientation, but inconsistency in the other two orientations. While their responses in the survey indicated more behaviorist and cognitivist beliefs, they might not truly believe that teaching reading in behaviorist and cognitivist orientations would be more effective than teaching reading in a constructivist orientation.

4   Conceptualization of the Interaction between the Two Stated Belief Systems

Through the analysis above, I reported diverse relationships (consistent or inconsistent) or interactions between stated beliefs about reading and stated beliefs about teaching reading among the participating teachers. In the section below, I provide the reader with a further analysis of these relationships or interactions through conceptualizing these two constructs (reading beliefs vs. reading teaching beliefs). Just like I did in the previous chapter, applying this kind of conceptualization makes it possible to draw theoretical implications and also offers a visualized way to present and interpret the interactions between the two constructs.

The analysis in this part entails three kinds of relationships between the teachers' stated beliefs about reading and their stated beliefs about teaching reading. The two constructs may develop individually, representing their initial conditions or emerging states. These initial conditions determine the way the two constructs interact and may also influence their convergence or divergence in a scalar way. Take the two constructs in the behaviorist orientation of the study as an example: the statistical analysis did not yield any correlation between the stated beliefs about reading and the stated beliefs about teaching reading. The two belief systems move and develop individually, without any converging tendency (see Figure 8).

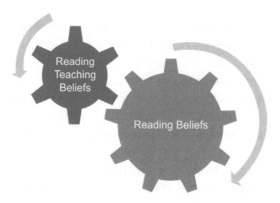

FIGURE 8
Two systems moving individually

The analysis also yielded insights for the second type of interaction between the two constructs; that is, the two constructs may develop toward each other and make attempts to interact (see Figure 9). For example, in the study, stated beliefs about reading and the beliefs about teaching reading in the cognitivist orientation, while not in a statistically significant relationship, still shared a great amount of correspondence (40.4%, as reported in Table 11).

There also exists another type of interaction between stated beliefs about reading and stated beliefs about teaching reading; namely, the two belief systems converge in a way that one informs the other. For example, in this study, the two systems of teachers' beliefs toward the dominant constructivist orientation showed a significant association, indicating a close interaction between them (see Figure 10).

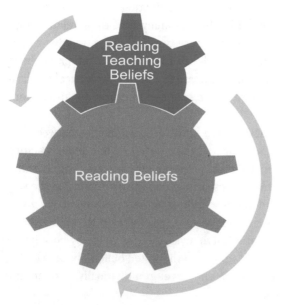

FIGURE 9
Two systems attempt to interact

FIGURE 10
Two systems interacting closely

It is worth mentioning that the three kinds of relationships between the two belief systems indicate three kinds of interactions. The interaction may start from an emerging state when two belief systems move individually, to the state when the two systems make attempts to interact, to the final state when the two systems manage to interact. However, technically, the two systems cannot totally overlap; pedagogical beliefs may to some extent lag behind the content area knowledge beliefs, as the latter can be seen as the prior experience or knowledge of the former. There might be other possible explanations for the interactions or relationships between the two belief systems beyond the ones stated in this chapter.

5   Conclusion

In this chapter, I attempted to describe the interactions between two types of belief systems through both statistical and qualitative analyses. Statistically, the two belief systems that leaned toward the constructivist orientation showed a significant association with it, and the belief systems that leaned toward the other two (the behaviorist or the cognitivist orientations) were without any significance. However, the interactions between the two systems were only limited to the dominant orientations, with much more to explore for the dual or multiple orientations in the future. I also offered possible explanations for the interaction, which to some extent entails a consistency between teachers' beliefs about reading and their beliefs about teaching reading. I ended the chapter with the conceptualization of the interactions between the two belief systems, arguing the two systems may develop from the emerging state to the interactive state. (In the next chapter, I will further explore and present how the two belief systems interact with actual practice, depicting a general picture of the belief-practice system.)

References

Bartlett, F. C. (1932). *Remembering*. Cambridge University Press.

Bernhardt, E. (1986). Cognitivist processes in L2: An examination of reading behaviors. In J. Lantolf & L. Labarca (Eds.), *Research in second language learning: Focus on the classroom* (pp. 35–51). Ablex.

Borg, S. (2003). Teacher cognition in language teaching: A review of research into what language teachers think, know, believe and do. *Language Teaching, 36*(2), 81–109.

Borg, S. (2006). *Teacher cognition and language education: Research and practice*. Continuum.

Borg, S. (2009). English language teachers' conceptions of research. *Applied Linguistics, 30*(3), 355–388.

Cambria, J., & Guthrie, J. T. (2010). Motivating and engaging students in reading. *The NERA Journal, 46*(1), 16–29.

Coady, J. (1979). A psycholinguistic model of the ESL reader. In R. Mackay, B. Barkman, & R. R. Jordan (Eds.), *Reading in a second language* (pp. 5–12). Newbury House.

Cortazzi, M., & Jin, L. X. (1996). Cultures of learning: Language classrooms in China. In H. Coleman (Ed.), *Society and the language classroom* (pp. 169–206). Cambridge University Press.

Creswell, J. W. (2009). *Research design: Qualitative, quantitative, and mixed methods approaches* (3rd ed.). Sage.

Creswell, J. W. (2012). *Qualitative inquiry and research design: Choosing among five traditions* (3rd ed.). Sage.

DeFord, D. (1978). *A validation study of an instrument to determine teachers' theoretical orientation to reading instruction* [PhD dissertation]. Indiana University.

Ertmer, P. A., & Newby, T. J. (2013). Behaviorism, cognitivism, constructivism: Comparing critical features from an instructional design perspective. *Performance Improvement Quarterly, 26*(2), 43–71.

Farrell, T. S. C. (1999). The reflective assignment: Unlocking pre-service English teachers' beliefs on grammar teaching. *RELC Journal, 30*(2), 1–17.

Gao, Y. (2013). Incorporating sociocultural theory into second language (L2) reading instruction: A unit plan for EFL learners. *US-China Foreign Languages, 11*(11), 859–869.

Gatbonton, E. (2008). Looking beyond teachers' classroom behavior: Novice and experienced ESL teachers' pedagogical knowledge. *Language Teaching Research, 12*(2), 161–182.

Goodman, K. (1967). Reading: A psycholinguistic guessing game. *Journal of the Reading Specialist, 6*(4), 126–135.

Goodman, K. (1986). *What's whole in whole language?* Heinemann Educational Books.

Gough, P. B. (1972). Theoretical models and processes of reading. In J. F. Kavanagh & I. G. Mattingly (Eds.), *Language by ear and by eye* (pp. 661–685). MIT Press.

Gough, P. B. (1993). The beginning of decoding. *Reading and Writing: An Interdisciplinary Journal, 5*(2), 181–192.

Gutierrez Almarza, G. (1996). Student foreign language teacher's knowledge growth. In D. Freeman & J. C. Richards (Eds.), *Teacher learning in language teaching* (pp. 50–78). Cambridge University Press.

Harasim, L. (2017). *Learning theory and online technologies* (2nd ed.). Routledge.

Harste, J. C., & Burke, C. L. (1977). A new hypothesis for reading teacher research: Both the teaching and learning of reading are theoretically based. In P. D. Pearson (Ed.), *Reading: Theory, research and practice* (pp. 32–40). National Reading Conference.

Hu, G. W. (2002). English language teaching in the People's Republic of China. In R. E. Silver, G. W. Hu, & M. Iino (Eds.), *English language education in China, Japan, and Singapore* (pp. 1–77). National Institute of Education.

Johnson, K. E. (1992). The relationship between teachers' beliefs and practices during literacy instruction for non-native speakers of English. *Journal of Reading Behavior, 24*(1), 83–108.

Kinzer, C. K. (1988). Instructional frameworks and instructional choices: Comparisons between preservice and in-service teachers. *Journal of Reading Behavior, 20*(4), 357–377.

Kırkgöz, Y. (2008). A case study of teachers' implementation of curriculum innovation in English language teaching in Turkish primary education. *Teaching and Teacher Education, 24*(7), 1859–1875.

LaBerge, D., & Samuels, S. (1974). Toward a theory of automatic information processing in reading. *Cognitivist Psychology, 6*(2), 293–323.

Larsen-Freeman, D., & Cameron, L. (2008). Research methodology on language development from a complex systems perspective. *The Modern Language Journal, 92*(2), 200–213.

Li, L. (2013). The complexity of language teachers' beliefs and practice: One EFL teacher's theories. *The Language Learning Journal, 41*(2), 175–191. https://doi.org/10.1080/09571736.2013.790132

Merriam, S. (1998). *Qualitative research and case study applications in education.* Jossey-Bass.

Morrison, T. G., Wilcox, B., Madrigal, J. L., Roberts, S., & Hintze, E. (1999). Teachers' theoretical orientations toward reading and pupil control ideology: A national survey. *Reading Research and Instruction, 38*(4), 333–350.

Ng, C., & Tang, E. (1997). Teachers' needs in the process of EFL reform in China – A report from Shanghai. *Perspectives: Working Papers, 9*(1), 63–85.

Ormrod, J. (2008). *Human learning* (5th ed.). Pearson.

Pajares, M. F. (1992). Teachers' beliefs and educational research: Cleaning up a messy construct. *Review of Educational Research, 62*(3), 307–332.

Peterson, B. E., & Williams, S. R. (1998). Mentoring beginning teachers. *Mathematics Teacher, 91*(8), 730–734.

Phipps, S., & Borg, S. (2009). Exploring tensions between teachers' grammar teaching beliefs and practices. *System, 37*(3), 380–390.

Rayner, K., & Pollatsek, A. (1989). *The psychology of reading.* Prentice Hall.

Reutzel, D., & Cooter, R. B. (1996). *Teaching children to read: From basals to books* (2nd ed.). Merrill/Prentice Hall.

Rosenblatt, L. M. (1994). The transactional theory of reading and writing. In R. B. Ruddell, M. R. Ruddell, & H. Singer (Eds.), *Theoretical models and processes of reading* (4th ed., pp. 1057–1092). International Reading Association.

Rumelhart, D. E. (1977). Understanding and summarizing brief stories. In D. Laberge & S. J. Samuels (Eds.), *Basic processes in reading* (pp. 265–303). Erlbaum.

Rumelhart, D. E. (1980). Schemata: The building blocks of cognition. In R. J. Spiro, B. C. Bruce, & W. F. Brewer (Eds.), *Theoretical issues in reading comprehension* (pp. 33–58). Erlbaum.

Shulman, L. S. (1986). Those who understand; Knowledge growth in teaching. *Educational Researcher, 15*(2), 4–14.

Skinner, B. F. (1938). *The behavior of organisms: An experimental analysis.* Appleton-Century.

Skott, J. (2001). The emerging practices of a novice teacher: The roles of his school mathematics images. *Journal of Mathematics Teacher Education, 4*(1), 3–28.

Smith, F. (1971). *Understanding reading.* Holt, Rinehart & Winston.

Stanovich, K. E. (1980). Toward an interactive-compensatory model of individual differences in the development of reading fluency. *Reading Research Quarterly, 16*(1), 32–71.

Vygotsky, L. S. (1978). *Mind in society: The development of higher psychological processes.* Harvard University Press.

Watson, J. B. (1913). Psychology as the behaviorist views it. *Psychological Review, 20*(2), 158–177.

Wilson, K. & Yang, L. (2007). A social constructivist approach to teaching reading: Turning the rhetoric into reality. *CELEA Journal, 30*(1), 1–6.

Yin, R. K. (2003). *Case study research: Design and methods.* Sage.

Zainal, Z. (2003). Critical review of reading model and theories in first and second language. *Human Journal/Jurnal Kemanusiaan, 1*(2), 104–124.

The Nexus of Chinese EFL Teachers' Beliefs and Practices

1 Introduction

The previous chapter provides a general picture of how quantitative data were analyzed in the study. In the quantitative section, statistical and descriptive analyses were conducted to answer Research Questions 1 and 2. In this qualitative analysis, I describe my data on teachers' classroom observations and integrate them with the findings from the survey responses. The whole process aimed at responding to Research Question 3: Are Chinese EFL teachers' beliefs about reading and teaching reading consistently observed in their actual practices? I used an abductive and iterative method to analyze the qualitative data (Dörnyei, 2007), which were generated from both classroom observations and survey responses about teaching beliefs. An abductive analysis entails a form of logical inference that starts with observations seeking the simplest and most likely explanation, while an iterative analysis is a process built on systematic and recursive repetition (Richardson & Kramer, 2006). As reported in the previous chapter, core and peripheral beliefs coexist in the belief system with multiple theoretical orientations to reading. A core belief was similar to a dominant belief; it outperformed peripheral beliefs in percentage and frequency in the belief system. This finding was in accordance with Borg's (2003, 2006, 2009) work on teacher cognition and practice.

Research Question 3: Are Chinese EFL Teachers' Beliefs about Reading and Teaching Reading Consistently Observed in Their Actual Practices?
While the teachers who participated in the quantitative survey were selected from three universities as the research sites, the seven participants in the qualitative section were selected from only one university due to the convenience and logistics in the observations. As the seven participants were from four different teaching faculty teams in the university, they were further grouped into four cases for the sake of better observation and analysis. The following section provides a detailed analysis of the seven participants' stated beliefs and actual practices. It then describes the qualitative findings in four cases.

© KONINKLIJKE BRILL NV, LEIDEN, 2022 | DOI: 10.1163/9789004506541_007

2   Purposive Participants

Purposive participants in the study were seven EFL teachers from the three selected universities. I chose these participants according to a few criteria. First, while the majority of the purposive participants were those teachers who showed inconsistency between their stated beliefs and practices, I still attempted to select one or two participants who demonstrated consistency between their stated beliefs and practices. In this way, I further developed the picture of what factors might trigger the (in)consistencies between the EFL teachers' stated beliefs and actual practices. Second, the selected participants were also the teachers who showed differences in other aspects, including years of experience, teaching English/non-English major students, gender, etc., which I assumed might trigger some inconsistencies between their teaching beliefs and practices. By doing so, further analysis of these factors helped me gain a clearer picture of what triggers inconsistencies between their teaching beliefs and practices. Third, these participants were evenly selected from the universities to test whether factors like their teaching sites are factors causing the inconsistencies. It is worth mentioning that the primary aim of the study is not to explore factors that might cause inconsistencies between stated beliefs and practices or inform the interactions between the two constructs. However, discussion of these factors would be part of the section focus, as it will lead the line of inquiry to develop for future studies.

The purposive participants in the qualitative part include seven teachers who were teaching college English in the research site. While the subjects were selected from three universities as the research sites, the seven participants in the qualitative part were selected only from one university due to the inconvenience of logistics and observations. As the seven participants were from four teaching faculty teams in the university, they were further grouped into four cases for the sake of better observations and analysis. Initial contact with the dean of the seven participants' affiliate helped me with some basic biographic or personality knowledge about them, which made the observation process easy.

Case 1 consisted of two teachers, one male, and one female. They were both emerging and young scholars. The male teacher Y had only two years of teaching experience, and the female teacher D had been teaching English in the research site for six years by the time of the research.

Case 2 consisted of two middle-aged teachers, S and L, who were both the team leaders of the teaching faculty teams in the university. As reported by the dean in their affiliate, S had great leadership skills and L was a teacher with great classroom management skills.

Case 3 was only one teacher, LY, who had been teaching English to college students for less than ten years. She did her master's degree in the United Kingdom and was the only teacher of the four cases who had a study-abroad experience. She was also a team leader in the teaching faculty team and was actively involved in some administrative work.

Case 4 included two female teachers, X and R, who were both in their 40s. As wives and mothers, they needed to maintain a balance between work and home life.

3   Within Case Findings

Case 1: Y & D, supporters, and implementers of dual, consistent reading/teaching beliefs. Two of the observed teachers expressed a dual reading belief system in their surveys and then applied their reading and reading teaching beliefs consistently to their actual practices in the classroom. For both teachers, the theoretical orientations comprised a dual belief system including behaviorism and cognitivism.

Beliefs about English reading and teaching reading. An analysis of the responses from the survey questions indicated that, statistically, those who held behaviorist and cognitivist reading beliefs did not necessarily hold teaching beliefs in the same domains. As the exceptions, Case 1 was particularly consistent in their beliefs; thus, their answers on teaching and reading often overlapped. Responses from both areas will be explored below to paint a comprehensive picture of their belief systems. Y, when asked to define reading in the survey, stated, "English reading means a lot to me. It is the best way to improve your comprehensive reading skills, enrich your vocabulary, and board [broaden] your horizon." He believed that language skills and vocabulary were the key points for defining English reading, which indicated a cognitivist (skill-based) and behaviorist (language units) reading model. For example, when asked how to help students solve problems they meet in reading, Y responded: "For words, I *insist* on teaching them the root, the prefix, and the suffix. For pronunciation, I teach them vowels and consonants one by one." The word "insist" in his response indicated his attitude toward the method he used to teach. The prefix-root-suffix pattern in word formation is a behaviorist way to view words as a combination of different linguistic units. Y also believed that vowels and consonants are important to students' pronunciation. The decision to teach these vowels and consonants "one by one" also indicated Y's belief that teaching is a mechanical process. Y further explained what he thinks would develop students' reading ability: "[F]irst and foremost, they *must* enhance their basic skills. For example, grammar and basic words." Again, his belief in teaching English words and grammar was indicated in his survey responses.

While Y acknowledged the role that language units play in a sentence, he also taught reading skills and focused on reading comprehension. These constructs served as cues of a cognitivist theoretical orientation. For example, when asked to define what good reading is, he stated that "good English reading can be divided into two aspects, including comprehensive reading and skimming and scanning." Y thought extensive reading and the read-aloud method were very important in a student's reading process.

His dual belief system regarding reading was also reflected in his survey response to the question "What should an English teacher do to help his/her student who does not read well?" He believed in three primary ways to help struggling EFL readers: the primary way was to "enhance their basic skills, for example, grammar and basic words." His clarification on what constitutes "basic skills" includes small language units, such as grammatical rules and basic words. The first step in his response indicated his perception of the importance of vocabulary in English reading (a behaviorist view). He went on: "The second step: try to understand the context. Third step: learn more background information." The second and third steps indicated a cognitivist orientation, as both context and background information are mediators to help students improve their reading comprehension. Because the other two methods were more cognitivist in nature, focusing on understanding, he exhibited a balanced approach between the two schools of thought.

Similar to Y, his colleague D defined English reading in three primary functions: "(1) Comprehension, (2) Searching for information, (3) One basic requirement of learning English." Comprehension – which is the focus of the cognitivist school (Goodman, 1967) – the emphasis on information-seeking and the perception of reading as a basic skill, illustrate that D's beliefs of reading instruction lie, at least in part, within a cognitivist orientation.

However, D's cognitivist beliefs were peripheral to her core behaviorist reading belief. For example, when asked how to define a good reader, she stated that a good English reader is someone who has "a good grasp of English vocabulary" and "a good understanding of English words." A good reader "knows every word in all kinds of material he reads and can understand it thoroughly." The emphasis on language units, especially vocabulary, evidenced D's behaviorist theoretical orientation. Therefore, for D, her perception and beliefs about English reading and reading instruction indicated both behaviorist and cognitivist orientations.

Like Y, D held behaviorist and cognitivist orientations, and her beliefs were indicated in her open-ended survey responses about defining and explaining both reading and teaching reading. For example, when asked what might be helpful strategies for reading, D answered: "Guess the meaning according to the context. If it hinders his understanding, look it up in the dictionary or search for information about it." The inferential method from the context indicated a cognitivist reading orientation, which equated making predictions through reading to a psychological guessing game or process (Goodman, 1967; Smith, 1971). The assistance from the dictionary indicated a focus on the phonemes and word meaning, both language cues in the behaviorist paradigm (Gough, 1972). D's beliefs represented a dual belief system, including both cognitivist and behaviorist tenets.

When asked how she, as a teacher, could help students improve their reading abilities, D stated that she would encourage students to enlarge their vocabularies and do more reading. She further suggested three primary strategies that would benefit her students in developing their reading: "1) Guess meaning from context. 2) Inspire students' learning interests. 3) [Increase/improve] [t]he communication between teachers and students about reading skills." Each of these practices has its roots in cognitivist theory. However, D's further response that reading interest should be built upon extensive reading led it back to a behaviorist orientation.

Observations of actual practice. Both Y and D held a dual belief system of behaviorism and cognitivism in both their reading and reading teaching beliefs. The following section presents how their stated beliefs were consistently indicated through observations of their actual practices.

Y, who frequently used decoding and direct teaching in his class, also emphasized vocabulary instruction and word-formation rules. The excerpt below was selected from his opening of a new lesson.

Q: Do you still remember at last class we have a test, right? In order to learn from the text, we get a review of them, okay? Let's get the review together. The first one, *identify*, do you still remember? With *identity*, we can get a root – *ident*. See another example, the word *credit*, and we have another word *credible*. And then you can see [inaudible], do you remember it?

A: Yes.

Q: *Vinc* means *to conquer*. And there is another very important word – anorexia. Do you know what does it mean?

A: Yeah.

Q: ... You have got it. And then supplement. Is it a verb or noun?

A: Verb.

Q: *Ment, ment.* It's a verb. I told you it's a verb. Okay. And we have the last phrase, *by all means*. Okay, so what's the meaning of *by all means*?

Y used typical, rote instructional methods to teach reading, including the decoding method. Right after he began his class, he used the lexical method, which describes a word in the form of prefix + root + suffix, to teach three words to students, i.e., the root "*ident*" in the paired words "identify-identity," the root "*vinc*," which means "to conquer," and the suffix "*ment*" in the word "supplement." Using a similar method, Y frequently divided phrases into their constituent parts. For example, he taught phrases such as "be into," "be/get involved in," and "a sense of" on a regular basis. After reading any single sentence, including typical phrases or collocations, he taught these phrases to the students. The following example is selected from the transcript:

> Yeah. She is unable in which aspect? "To be 'thin' began to torture me." Okay, you remember the meaning, it's very good. "I found myself involved in the competition again." We have learned "involved in," right? In paragraph three, she says that she is always involved in competitions – dancing, horseback riding. And then "but this time, I was competing against myself." She competed with herself. Against is a preposition. You can remember this sentence.

Y taught the text paragraph by paragraph in a bottom-up decoding approach. Additionally, for every paragraph, students were asked to read aloud. All those methods indicated a behaviorist orientation (Morrison et al., 1999; Zainal, 2003). However, there were still cognitivist aspects to his teaching style. One example that illustrated how Y held dual belief systems is that when he taught a specific concept, he encouraged students to go back and forth in the text to look for clues that led to the comprehension of a certain concept. For example:

> Yes, there is no perfection. Right? And we know the background – the author wants to achieve perfection, in paragraph one. In paragraph two, we see there is a very useful phrase called "a supportive family." It means the family condition is very good. Why does the author not use "a rich family" here? Think about it. If I say he has a very rich family, it just means his family has a lot of money, very wealthy, but it cannot indicate the moral or ethical part of the family. Okay, let's go on. In paragraph three, I want to ask you several words. And the second line, she says, "I was into acting by age seven." So, what does "was into" mean?

The first few sentences painted a picture of how Y was leading his students to what they had learned in the previous paragraphs to review a concept and then associate that concept with new knowledge. This method is based on the cognitivist belief that schemata were important in one's comprehension of a certain concept (Goodman, 1967; Smith, 1971). However, at the end of the excerpt, he again focused on an individual word or phrase ("was into"), which indicated a behaviorist orientation (Gough, 1972).

D, conversely, exhibited few if any cognitivist practices during my observation of her. She used the translation method (a form of decoding) to let her students translate the words or phrases from their first language (L1) into a second language (L2) and vice versa. As a behaviorist, D focused on the integration of language skills, which indicated a skill-based reading model (Morrison et al., 1999; Rosenblatt, 1994; Stanovich, 1980). For example, when she was guiding the students to analyze paragraph structure, she taught students how to use supporting details or examples to prove their argument and thus improve their writing. In addition, D taught the past tense or past/present participle of a word on a regular basis in her class in order to encourage memorization, which further indicated a decoding way of teaching reading.

Observations of consistency between beliefs and actual practice. Y and D both exhibited a behaviorist beliefs core and a peripheral cognitivist belief. The primary purpose of reading, in their stated beliefs, was to seek information, learn language units or segments, and comprehend a reading text. The participants comprising Case 1 further believed that reading was primarily composed of language cues, including words or phrases, and teaching reading meant to teach students these cues. Their stated teaching beliefs prioritized direct/rote instruction, the translation method, the decoding approach, word-formation rules, and focus-on-form.

They also believed that guiding students to comprehend a text was important in developing students' reading ability, evidencing a significant cognitivist viewpoint. However, while they expressed their belief that understanding a text was necessary, they believed it was relatively less important than teaching vocabulary, phrases, or sentence structures to their students, thus leaving that belief on the periphery of their behaviorist framework. They believed that students could understand the text as a whole only when they first understood all the individual words or sentences. The two teachers showed consistency between their stated beliefs and actual practices.

Case 2: S and L, advocates of multiple reading beliefs but practitioners of a dual belief system. In contrast to Y and D, other teachers showed inconsistencies between their stated beliefs and classroom practices. S and L, the participants in Case 2, indicated a multiple reading belief system in their surveys but then practiced a dual belief system in their reading instruction. Because they differed in their responses, in the following sections I will discuss them individually before analyzing their differences and similarities.

S's beliefs about reading. S indicated a dual belief system about English reading. S defined English reading as "[t]he process of using *English words to obtain information*. A cognitivist process which involves using previous knowledge to enhance language learning." The focus on English words, information seeking, and cognitivist processes indicated that S held both behaviorist and cognitivist theoretical orientations. S believed that language units, particularly words, were the medium through which a reader can search for information.

When asked how to define good English reading, S stated: "[G]ood English reading entails [knowing] the *general structure of a text*, the main idea of each paragraph in a given discourse." The response indicated a whole-language approach that emphasized the structure of a text as a whole (Anderson & Pearson, 1984; Rumelhart, 1980). He also believed that "[a] good reader should have *an extensive vocabulary, solid background knowledge,* and *the passion to acquire information through English media. A* good English reader can *solve his/her problem independently*." This response indicated multiple theoretical orientations: e.g., a large vocabulary showed a behaviorist orientation, a solid background knowledge represented a cognitivist paradigm, and the passion and problem-solving ability indicated a constructivist belief system. His beliefs in a cognitivist orientation also appeared in his definitions of good reading and a good reader, whereas his beliefs in the other two orientations only appeared in the latter. Thus, three orientations coexisted in his belief system; his constructivist and behavior orientations were peripheral compared to the core cognitivist beliefs indicated in his response.

S's beliefs regarding reading instruction. While S exhibited a belief in multiple theoretical orientations (all three) when defining English reading and readers, he did not include constructivism in his ideas about how reading instruction should be provided to EFL students. His core beliefs were both behaviorist and cognitivist. He believed that direct instruction, understanding of the cognitivist process of reading, and effective reading skills are important and helpful to EFL learners in a behaviorist orientation. He also believed that students should be taught how to comprehend the main ideas within each paragraph and identify the general structure of an essay.

Moreover, he believed that inter-thinking, brainstorming, and consideration of unity and coherence were also crucial for EFL learners. These areas of focus indicated a cognitivist orientation in their emphasis on understanding (Anderson & Pearson, 1984; Morrison et al., 1999; Rumelhart, 1980). He also felt that "a good vocabulary and culture background knowledge are of crucial importance to his EFL students," putting him within the behaviorist orientation as well.

L's beliefs about reading. L also held a dual theoretical orientation that included behaviorism and constructivism. For example, in her definitions of English reading/good English reading, she stated:

> It's a way to *acquire knowledge* and perceive the world in another language besides your mother tongue. And as a second language learner, it also helps to *improve language proficiency.* ... Good English reading is *a process* in which readers can fully understand the content in details. The reader can get the theme as well as *the author's intention.* At the same time, readers can *appreciate the beauty* of English writing.

She focused on reading skills/strategies, language proficiency, and content details that indicated a behaviorist orientation when defining a good reader. She also acknowledged affective factors like communication between reader and writer and aesthetic appreciation of the language, etc., which indicated that meaning was constructed between reader and writer and between reader and text in a constructivist orientation (Ertmer & Newby, 2013; Stanovich, 1980). When asked to give an example of an ideal good reader, she mentioned a friend of hers who read easily and was capable of quickly comprehending content material. She also believed her friend to be a good reader because he read out of joy and pleasure, not out of obligation. This focus on content and holistic understanding was held by the constructivist school. She indicated her behaviorist orientation by highlighting reading fluency and the importance of extensive reading – both mechanical processes of reading (Gough, 1972; LaBerge & Samuels, 1974).

L's beliefs about reading instruction. Unlike S, L's stated beliefs of reading in a dual behaviorist and constructivist way were indicated consistently in her stated beliefs about teaching reading. For example, when asked how to help students solve problems met in reading a text, she said:

> If it is an unfamiliar word, s/he can easily find it *in a dictionary* or even just neglect it. But for the understanding of a sentence or a point, a good reader *may repeat reading it or go on reading and then try to understand it in a larger context.*

L believed that understanding the text using context is helpful in solving EFL students' problems. She reported other strategies to help her EFL students as well. For example, she felt strongly about the importance of consistently practicing key skills; this kind of belief mirrors the stimulus-and-response theory of B. F. Skinner, a typical representative of behaviorism who influenced the reading field by highlighting the mechanical process of reading (Gough, 1972; LaBerge & Samuels, 1974). Together with these behaviorist beliefs, L felt that a constructivist philosophy could also help her students. She said, "to find out the problem s/he has in reading and give s/he [him/her] suggestions according to the problem, such as *enlarging vocabulary* [*and*] *improving reading skills*." She used a case-by-case analysis and a suggestion-instead-of-solution way to guide her students.

L's *beliefs about reading instruction.* Her multiple beliefs about reading were revealed in her survey responses. For example, when asked how she could help her students improve their reading proficiency, she stated:

> I'd like to pose questions before their reading. Students will find the answers during their reading. *These questions will help them to understand both details and [the] main ideas of the text.* After that, I'd like to help students understand the merits of this writing.

Her primary reason for using guiding questions was to help her students grasp the main ideas and details within the text. In her further explanation of why she found such strategies helpful, she stated that through guiding questions, her class covered most English reading skills. Again, this skill-focused belief indicated a cognitivist orientation (Goodman, 1967). The last question in the survey was, "What is the most important factor in teaching reading?" L responded:

> I think the most important [factor] in teaching reading is to *help students improve English proficiency as well as their interest in reading.* They can get information quickly if they want it. They can also enjoy reading a great piece of work in their spare time.

Her belief in the behaviorist orientation was indicated in this response ("improving language proficiency"), which also indicated behaviorism via a focus on the language cues (Gough, 1972). In addition, "arousing the student interest" is a tenet of constructivism, which highlighted the affective factors and scaffolding function in reading (Stanovich, 1980).

S and L's methods used in actual practice. In practice, both S and L showed a preference for teaching reading in a hybrid way, with behaviorist and constructivist reading orientations involved. As in Case 1, the cognitivist viewpoint was not apparent. S and L both believed that leading students to associate reading excerpts with their own experiences or with real-world problems was important. For example, in S's class, when he taught the phrase "deep and shallow" to his students majoring in navigation engineering, he prompted them to think about a situation they might actually encounter:

> For example, if you work onboard the ship and become the first officer and the second officer, like you. You will direct your ship and navigate the ship just along the coast area, right? Usually, the coast area is very shallow. It's not so deep enough.

While S used real-world association (a constructivist method) on a regular basis in his class, he also adopted the decoding method to teach English words to his students. For example, he taught students to distinguish paired words like "wonder-wander" and "alone-lonely." The way he led students to distinguish language units like phonemes and morphemes indicated his behaviorist orientation of instruction. Similarly, S asked students to make sentences with given words, chop sentences into pieces, and arrange single pieces in sequence to better their understanding.

While S used both orientations on a regular basis, the dominant methods used in the classroom were of a constructivist orientation, particularly in the instances when he cited real-world examples. Sometimes, however, the two orientations were difficult to distinguish. For example, when he explained the phrase "seven seas" to his students, he said:

> What are the seven seas? I think here seven is not definitely a number. Seven just means many. Just like in China, we say cloud nine and the eighteenth hell. So that number is not exact, right? So just take it as so many. So, all the waters – remember, I have told you water is an uncountable noun, right? Anyway, when we mention this word, waters in maritime English indicate different ... just the areas of water. Indian Ocean, Atlantic Ocean, Pacific Ocean, maybe [inaudible]. So, it is different areas of water. In Chinese, we can say *shui yu*. It is different areas of water in maritime English. Here, seven seas, I think, mean different areas and different waters. Although they are different areas, they connect with each other, right? Yes or no?

At the surface level, S used some behaviorist orientations. Specifically, he used Chinese-English association and translation and focused on the class of the word (e.g., whether it is a countable or uncountable noun). The primary purpose of these methods was to figure out the meaning of the word. However, further analysis of his teaching methods indicated that he was actually guiding the students to associate their new knowledge (the idiom of "the seven seas") with their current knowledge (water's uncountability and the Chinese phrase *shui yu*), a process more easily identified as constructivist.

Similar to S, L also used a hybrid of behaviorist and constructivist orientations to teaching reading, omitting the cognitivist orientation she demonstrated in her survey responses. Key behaviorist examples included her use of diction at the beginning of the class to reinforce students' memorization of key lexical items. She paid particular attention to students' spelling and correct use of parts of speech. For example, she asked the students to figure out whether a word was a noun or an adjective on a regular basis in her class. L analyzed almost the entire text sentence by sentence, phrase by phrase. A frequent signal phrase she used while teaching was "XXX means XXX," and a typical instructional method she frequently used is read-aloud, both of which fall into the behaviorist category.

Also, like S, L used constructivist methods to associate students' learning with real-world experiences. For example, when she introduced concepts from e-commerce, she asked students to think about their actual shopping experiences. The tools she used to guide the students to internalize their knowledge and construct meaning indicated a constructivist orientation (Morrison et al., 1999; Rosenblatt, 1994; Stanovich, 1980).

L frequently associated concepts with real-world experiences in her class. Besides the above-mentioned e-commerce example, L also led students to discuss their feelings about watching American TV series, e.g., *The Walking Dead* and *The Big Bang Theory*. The purpose was for students to discuss the effects that TV series might have on people's lives and what kind of plots the students found interesting. She used all these activities to lead students to speak in English. Compared to S, L more frequently talked about the text as a whole and used more association methods to lead students to speak aloud and discuss it. During the observation period, the time allocated to students for peer discussion and group work in L's class was more than that in S's class.

While the two teachers used similar dual-oriented, interactive ways of teaching, they did have differences in their methods. While both teachers used constructivist orientations, L's use of constructivist methods was more frequent than S's. Except for the dictation activity L used at the beginning of her class, she seldom used any behaviorist methods. Conversely, while S did hold a dominant constructivist orientation in his teaching practice, he used more behaviorist methods than L did in the classroom.

Inconsistency between beliefs and actual practice. In classroom observations, S and L both showed an inconsistent attitude between their beliefs and their practices. While they both held a multiple reading belief system in their stated reading and teaching beliefs, they acted in dual theoretical orientations in their actual practices. To be more specific, both S and L believed in behaviorist, cognitivist, and constructivist theoretical orientations in their survey responses. However, when they taught their students in the actual classroom, they taught in an interactive way between behaviorism and constructivism. Their frequent use of constructivist methods in actual practice was not indicated in their stated beliefs about either reading or teaching reading.

In terms of their stated beliefs about reading and teaching reading, S's survey results indicated an inclination toward all three reading orientations. For example, in the survey, he stated: "a large vocabulary" represented a behaviorist orientation, "a solid background knowledge" represented a cognitivist orientation, and "the passion and problem-solving ability" represented a constructivist belief system. However, classroom observation indicated that a constructivist orientation was peripheral, compared to the core, cognitivist beliefs in his response.

However, with reference to his actual practice, S acted in a constructivist way by using interactive activities such as thinking aloud and association. While S used real-world association methods on a regular basis in his class, he also adopted the decoding method to teach English words to his students. In other words, he believed that in regard to beliefs, the constructivist orientation was core, and the behaviorist orientation was peripheral.

Similar to S, L also showed an imbalance in her way of teaching. She used more constructivist methods like an association with real-world experiences. For example, L used case-by-case analysis and suggestion-instead-of-solution methods to guide students. Her survey responses indicated that behaviorism and cognitivism informed her of how to define reading and helpful reading strategies. In her explanation on why the strategies she had mentioned were useful, she stated that these strategies cover most of the skills in English reading. She indicated a cognitivist orientation.

L also used a constructivist method to associate students' learning with real-world experiences. The method of associating concepts with real-world experiences was frequently used in L's classroom. Compared with the behaviorist methods, she used far more constructivist methods in the class. L's actual practice indicated that she held a core constructivist orientation with a peripheral behaviorist belief system. The dual belief system observed in her actual practice was not consistent with what she stated in the survey response.

Case 3: LY, contradictions among reading beliefs, teaching beliefs, and actual practice. LY indicated several inconsistencies. More specifically, there was inconsistency between her reading beliefs and teaching beliefs, as well as between her beliefs and practices.

Beliefs about reading. LY indicated a dual belief system in defining English reading. She believed that English reading was closely connected with reading skills. When asked to define English reading, LY defined it as "the most important skill for English." However, together with this cognitivist orientation (defining reading through a skill perspective), LY also acknowledged the "eye-broadening, entertaining and time-killing" function of reading. This indicated a constructivist orientation.

The dual belief system in her definition of English reading was also present in her responses to other survey questions. For example, when asked how to define "good reading," she stated that "good reading enables its readers to get something in a relaxing and entertaining way." This response conveyed two layers of meaning. Reading enables readers to receive information (a behaviorist orientation), and reading should also occur in a relaxing and entertaining way (a constructivist orientation). Her statement that "a patient, perseverant person who loves English can make a good reader" indicated both behaviorist and constructivist orientations, too. Her use of the ideas of *patience* and *perseverance* indicated a behaviorist belief in the importance of practice and repetition. However, the attributive clause "who loves English" indicated a constructivist orientation, as affection plays an important role in making a great reader.

Beliefs about teaching reading. When asked how to help a student who cannot read well, LY suggested: "[T]ry to select some proper material for him/her and help him/her develop a solid foundation or language skills first." Her beliefs regarding learning vocabulary within a text indicated a behaviorist orientation. LY believed that looking up words in a dictionary or online – in her own words, "check something on the internet; look through books to figure out the meaning" – would be effective, instead of reading the passage as a whole to guess the word meanings.

In contrast, LY also expressed her belief about reading instruction in a constructivist way: "Reading I thought was not taught. A teacher's role should be encouraging students to develop an interest in books and want to learn more. So, I choose to encourage and give pressure to students to read as much as possible." LY's interpretation of a teacher's role in teaching reading indicated a constructivist model. She preferred to guide students rather than merely teach them to read (Stanovich, 1980). She believed that being a guide or facilitator instead of a teacher or instructor was more meaningful for a reading teacher. In her own words, reading "was not taught."

When asked whether the methods she had proposed for teaching reading were effective, LY indicated that the effectiveness of those methods depends on the students and teachers. She believed it should be examined *case by case* rather than with a *one-size-fits-all* approach. She further restated that "encouraging students to read" was central to good reading instruction.

Methods used in actual practice. LY's teaching methods included all three orientations. She spent more time, however, on methods from the cognitivist orientation models in her actual practice. For instance, she focused on students' comprehension and understanding of vocabulary and text and used association – e.g., asking students to picture a certain concept in their minds to better their understanding of the concept. For an example, see the following excerpt:

> T: How do you understand *scary*?
> S: *Xia ren de.*
> T: Something is fearful, something is frightening, something that they can make her feel terrified. Do you remember the word *terrified*? She found terrified. She was fearful about her childhood. What do you know about your childhood? If you will use one word to describe your childhood, what do you use to describe this? Everyone thinks about this. What do you feel about your childhood?

LY first focused on language units, e.g., the word *scary*. However, she then asked students to associate the concept with real-world experience. This indicated her focus on the comprehension and understanding of the concept instead of specific words.

LY's focus on students' understanding of concepts or text was also indicated in her efforts to check students' understanding of every individual sentence throughout the entire text. Although LY used mostly cognitivist methods, she also adopted other methods like read-aloud, decoding, and phonic analysis to teach words in her class. These methods indicated a behaviorist orientation (Gough, 1993). Sometimes LY used sentence paraphrasing and translation methods, and other times she asked guiding questions, which were also behaviorist strategies.

> Now, the last sentence, which is also the key sentence. "I want everyone's praise." Not prize. So, what does *praise* mean? *Praise* means people say *you are doing well, well done*, and *acceptance. Acceptance* means people acknowledge your performance. "But as my own toughest," toughest the simple form of which is tough. OK, so what is *tough*? Can you say something? *Hard.* It's *hard* or sometimes very *strong*. You are a *tough* guy. You are a *tough* guy because you are not afraid of any difficulties. OK, this is a part. Here is the sentence: "as *my own toughest critic.*" What is a *critic*?

> When you see *critic*, you mean you are *critical* and *picky*. That means you
> are satisfied or not?

The method she used here was very structured. She guided students to learn
almost every new word in the sentence and also led students to read aloud on
a regular basis.

Mismatch between beliefs and actual practice. Compared to Case Studies 1 and
2, LY indicated more inconsistencies between her stated beliefs and practice.
In terms of beliefs about reading, LY had a multiple reading belief system that
included all three orientations. While she leaned more toward a constructivist
orientation, she maintained beliefs in the other two orientations. However, the
multiple beliefs she held in her stated responses about defining reading were
not consistently indicated in her stated belief about teaching reading. Instead
of a multiple belief system, LY indicated a constructivist orientation as her
core belief and a behaviorist orientation as the sole peripheral belief.

In terms of actual practice in the classroom, LY used more behaviorist and
cognitivist methods, which were different from the orientation indicated in
her stated responses about teaching reading. More specifically, in her stated
beliefs about teaching reading, LY indicated a constructivist orientation, which
helped foster students' interest in reading and set up teachers as guides or facilitators. However, in actual practice, LY was more instructor than facilitator. She
used more rote instruction and read-aloud methods. Therefore, inconsistencies between her stated beliefs about teaching reading and her actual practice
were indicated.

Another inconsistency was also indicated. LY demonstrated a prioritization
of behaviorist models in her actual practice, which contradicted the multiple
beliefs stated in her responses about defining reading. Despite her statement
that she valued constructivist, behaviorist, and cognitivist orientations, LY
hardly used the first in the classroom.

*Case 4: X and R, advocates of a dual belief system but practitioners of multiple
beliefs. X's reading beliefs.* X defined English reading as "a way to obtain information, entertainment or wisdom through visual capability in the language of
English." Information-seeking and processing were two of the primary functions he noted for English reading. Moreover, the acquisition of entertainment
and wisdom through language was also important. While emphasizing information-seeking and processing indicated cognitivist reading beliefs, appreciation of language in an entertaining way indicated a constructivist orientation.
In other words, both cognitivist and constructivist orientations were indicated
in her stated beliefs about reading and teaching reading. Other excerpts further indicated mixed orientations. For example, when asked to define "what is

good English reading?" X answered that "[i]t means a non-native speaker has the ability to understand the meaning of an article efficiently and form some mental exchange with the author." Apart from the textual understanding that indicated a cognitivist orientation, a mental exchange between reader and writer that indicated the constructivist orientation was also present.

When asked what makes a good reader, X stated that interest or intrinsic motivation shaped a great reader and even made one "excel" in his/her field. The way she interpreted a good reader indicated a constructivist view about English reading. She believed affective factors rather than repeated behaviors contributed to a great reader. X's constructivist beliefs were also indicated when explaining what strategies a good reader might use to solve problems he/she meets when reading a text. She believed that a good reader might utilize resources such as the internet, a dictionary, or relevant persons to solve those problems. These resources acted as different mediators in helping the reader determine how he/she can solve the problems. Learning mediators are an embodiment of sociocultural theories (Vygotsky, 1978). Researchers (e.g., Lantolf, 2000; Stanovich, 1980) posited that learners construct meanings of the world by communicating with different mediators.

X's beliefs about reading instruction. In terms of stated beliefs about teaching reading, X indicated a preference for constructivist methods. The strong influence of affective factors that she reported would comfort students and promote their development of critical reading skills.

In written responses on how, as a teacher, she can help readers to enhance their reading ability or solve problems they encounter while reading, X classified students into different groups and gave them different strategies on how they could improve their abilities and reading skills. This method of differentiating students and giving different groups different strategies is an indicator that X leaned toward a constructivist orientation.

However, X indicated a cognitivist orientation when asked to explain reading instruction. For example, apart from student differentiation strategies, X also believed that helping students to "analyze the structure of the long sentences" and to "find out the organization of an article" was important.

X's methods in actual practice. While X stated both cognitivist and constructivist beliefs in her written responses to survey questions, most of the instructional methods used in her class were behaviorist. For example, she frequently used methods like reading aloud, paraphrasing, word formation, and pattern drills. More specifically, X asked her students to read aloud every paragraph of the text before providing further instruction. She also led students to read aloud each new word with her from a word list. She also used dictation as a way to examine her students' memorization of words. The following excerpt is selected from the transcription of her observation, which indicated her behaviorist way of teaching reading:

> This is such a structure, and it can be used in adverbial [senses]. This is exactly in this case. In this article, you can find a lot of such kinds of structures. The second sentence is "He knows her heart but has never seen her." His interest began twelve months ago in a Florida library. If we write this sentence, it always begins with "he began to be interested in the girl with a rose." When you are writing, you can't always use the personal pronoun as the subject. It is too boring. In your homework, the beginning is always "I, I, I." So, this sentence is very flexible. The next sentence [inaudible]. In this sentence, pay attention firstly to [inaudible]. The "find" can be followed by the reflexive pronoun, like "yourself." It can be added [to] many elements. The first one is "found yourself" in the past tense. It can also be [a] present participle like red words in the introduction part. The adjective is OK. The prepositional phrase is allowed. For example, "I found myself involved in such a scandal." Anyway, it is "find yourself" plus past participle. Or, "I found myself sleeping in the English class." And "I found myself unable to follow the English teacher." It is the adjective. When he is awake, "he found himself in the hospital." It is the prepositional phrase. Anyway, "find yourself" can plus many different elements. The second sentence is "completely absorb my attention." It means to attract somebody completely.

The above excerpt indicated X's behaviorist orientation of teaching in a number of ways. First, X taught the paragraph in a decoding way, and chopped the text into sentences. Second, she focused on teaching grammatical components or language units in the text, e.g., the adverb, adjective, and prepositional clause. In addition, X broke down almost every sentence for the students to increase their understanding. Individually and collectively, these methods indicated a behaviorist orientation.

X used some cognitivist and constructivist ways to teach reading in her class, albeit infrequently. For example, when she started teaching a unit about love, she designed a warm-up activity by asking students to name three merits that their Mr./Mrs. Right in the future should possess. Then, she asked two volunteer students to write down all the students' responses on the blackboard and group the data into three top categories. Through this activity, students were able to summarize and learn many adjectives that are used to describe a person's characteristics and features. Students associated their real-world experience with the topic and then began learning the new text, which was a more constructivist approach.

R's reading beliefs. Similar to X, R also held mixed beliefs about reading and teaching reading. R believed reading was a process used to find the information a person is interested in. Both information seeking (Gough, 1972) and mental development (Goodman, 1967, 1986) were indicated in her stated beliefs, which showed both behaviorist and constructivist reading orientations. When asked to define what English reading is, R stated:

> English reading to me means a lot: primarily, it means to *find the information* I'm interested in from the reading materials; it also means a way to *broaden my horizons, cultivate my taste,* and *make me pleased and relaxed.*

R's answer to the question includes two key pieces of information. First, she believed that reading was a way to *collect* and *process* information (Goodman, 1967). This indicated a *cognitivist orientation.* Second, R believed that mental development and pleasure also are important results of reading, which is constructivist in nature.

Then, R explained what a good reader is: "A good reader can fully understand the author's intention of writing; appreciate the beauty of original works; [and] read as much as possible." This definition indicated a mixed-belief system – a cognitivist focus on author meaning and a constructivist goal of appreciation and intrinsic motivation. Specifically, she believed that constructing text meaning by communicating with the author was the primary way to define a good reader. This indicated a constructivist view (Stanovich, 1980; Zainal, 2003). R also believed that affective factors, including the appreciation of the text and the motivation to read extensively, were also qualities (traditionally tied to constructivism) that a great reader should have.

When asked to provide an example of a good reader in her actual life, R stated that one of her colleagues was a professor of English in her department, and he was a great reader in her mind. She explained, "[H]e has good command of English and he is interested in English literature. ... [H]e is knowledgeable, and he enjoys extensive reading of books of different kinds." R held a dual reading belief system, according to her stated beliefs. The constructivist beliefs were core beliefs, and cognitivist beliefs were the peripheral beliefs.

R's beliefs about reading instruction. When asked about ways to solve problems students encountered in reading, R stated that a combination of "search[ing] for the relevant background knowledge on the internet," "communicating with the author," and/or "consulting the professionals in this area" were great ways to address problems. R tended to solve problems through different mediators (books/internet, peers, and professors), a tendency embodying sociocultural theory (Lantolf, 2000).

Her constructivist beliefs about teaching reading were also indicated in her responses to what might be the best strategies to do so. Overall, R liked to differentiate students and give them different reading strategies. The way she organized her answers indicated a constructivist orientation:

> First, to find out his/her problems; for the problem concerning vocabulary, tell the student to consult the dictionary or try to guess its meaning in the context; for the problem concerning grammar, advise the student to practice more on the basic learning. For difficult articles, raise some questions concerning the reading, let students read with these questions [in mind]; for easy articles, organize the discussion after reading, discuss the uncertain places so that students can fully understand the reading material.

R believed that classifying students, problems, and reading materials was the first step in determining strategies. She believed that different reading assignments and strategies should be given to different students. R used "guiding questions, peer discussion, and checking through dictionary, all those constructivist methods should be mingled together into the remedy [for] students' reading problems." R's answer indicated a constructivist view of how reading instruction should be conducted.

Her constructivist beliefs about reading instruction were also indicated in her answer to the question, "What might be great reading instruction?" R stated:

1. Pay more attention to the interaction with students, discuss with the students
2. Help students with the understanding of the long and difficult sentences
3. Introduce the background knowledge about the American and British culture, writing features of Western people; instill such ideas constantly when teaching.

R also believed that interaction, peer discussion, and cultural context were important in reading instruction. Her stated beliefs indicated a constructivist orientation. She highlighted the notion that meaning and learning were constructed through peer interaction and discussion (Lantolf, 2000; Vygotsky, 1978; Zainal, 2003).

R also showed a cognitivist view in her ideas about reading with students. For example, she believed that reading instruction should "make students fully understand the reading materials" and "have a better understanding of Western people's writing purpose and writing techniques." She focused on reading comprehension and culture in teaching. In terms of why she thought teaching culture was helpful to students' comprehension, she stated: "[W]hen reading similar articles next time, students can accept the idea more easily."

R's methods in actual practice. R used instructional methods that indicated a behaviorist orientation more than the other two orientations, though all three made an appearance. R used four methods in her class: (1) grammar knowledge instruction, such as the attributive clause and adverbial clause; (2) sentence-making method, e.g., when she asked students to make sentences with the given words or phrases; (3) translation, e.g., when she guided students to translate words or sentences from Chinese to English and vice versa; and (4) word formation, such as how she taught students to divide a word into constituent morphemes. She used cognitivist and constructivist methods in her class infrequently.

R was the only teacher observed teaching phonics. For example, when she emphasized spelling, she often articulated the relevant phonemes:

> There are two S's in the word *profession*. Some students just write one. And *professional*. The latter one is *sense*, but some students wrote "professionals." The two are wrong. They are *profession, professional,* and *sense.* Another word that you [typically] just miss one letter is *impression.*

In order to help students memorize those words, R highlighted some spelling mistakes students typically made when writing. The letter-word structure indicated a decoding and phonics way of teaching reading, focusing on language cues or phonemes (Gough, 1972; DeFord, 1978). This is consistent with the behaviorist orientation.

Outside of grammar and spelling, R used a holistic approach to teaching in her class. She liked to analyze the whole structure of the text she was teaching and guide students to guess or infer meanings of certain sentences or paragraphs. For example, she said:

> Okay, now we see the article. We don't see the picture. Let's look at the passage. The first part is the first paragraph. What does the author tell us here? It's the hero of the story – John [inaudible]. He was a soldier. How can we tell? He was in army uniform. ...
>
> From paragraph two to paragraph six is the second part. What does this part introduce? It's about how these two people know each other and love each other. John has fallen in love with Mrs. [inaudible]. It introduces the process – how to meet and love each other.

Paragraph two, he knew this girl whose heart [inaudible] but whose face he didn't. The girl is with a rose. The girl is very good. How to say a heart like the gold?

Her analysis of the structure of the text indicated a constructivist orientation, focused on the meaning and message the author was trying to convey. She also used many guiding questions in teaching. She viewed herself as a facilitator rather than simply as an instructor. Also, the way she analyzed the text structure indicated a cognitivist orientation. She saw the whole structure of the text as a schema and taught students to pay attention to the structure. In addition, R also indicated the cognitivist view in her practice, as in the following:

> *Soul* has two meanings: one is the soul, and the other is human. It is totally silent and dead; there may not be any single soul on the street. *Thoughtful* means careful and kind. Her heart is careful and kind. If we say somebody is of great insight, we mean that somebody can observe deeply. It's during the Second World War when women played all kinds of characters. Have you ever seen the movies of Marilyn Monroe? She usually plays a beautiful blonde and acts like a vase. She doesn't have much intelligence. But here, the lady is insightful. So, we should value people's mind instead of appearance. Do you know anything about Marilyn Monroe? You know a little about the movie star.

R taught students to differentiate literal meanings from connotative meanings of a single word (vase, soul, etc.). She held a behaviorist orientation in using this method. She also introduced some relevant cultural knowledge or background information of the paragraph in order to better students' understanding of the content, all of which were cognitivist in nature.

R indicated a multiple reading belief system in actual practice. She indicated all three reading orientations in her practice.

Mismatch between beliefs and actual practice. For both X and R, their stated beliefs about reading and teaching reading were inconsistent with their actual practices. While they held a dual belief system that consisted of only behaviorist and constructivist orientations, they taught in a way that combined all three reading beliefs. Compared with X, R used more behaviorist instructional methods, such as word formation and translation. X, while having used methods that represented cognitivist and constructivist orientation, used more behaviorist methods.

The stated survey responses and classroom observations indicated that X and R alone showed more theoretical orientations in their actual practice than in their stated survey responses. The other teachers showed fewer theoretical orientations in their actual practice than in their responses.

4 Cross-Case Analysis

In addition to the within-case analysis, a cross-case analysis was also conducted. The purpose of the cross-case analysis was to investigate similarities and differences among stated beliefs about reading, beliefs about teaching reading, and actual practices across four case groups (see Table 13).

4.1 Stated Beliefs: Similarities vs. Differences

The observed teachers showed certain notable similarities and differences in terms of their stated beliefs in the survey responses.

Similarities. Three similarities about the participants' stated beliefs were indicated in the cross-case analysis. First, each of the three subbelief systems coexisted with at least one other within the belief structures stated and observed in participants. Classroom observations from all the selected case study groups indicated a coexistence among the three reading orientations. However, the distribution among the orientations was uneven; each teacher demonstrated behaviorist methods in their practice, but not in every teacher's beliefs. These qualitative findings corresponded to the quantitative result.

To expand on this overlap, a few of the observed teachers indicated a dominant reading belief model in their stated responses. Most teachers held a dual belief system. For example, Y and D both held dual belief systems about reading that included behaviorist and cognitivist orientations. Their dual stated beliefs about reading were then mirrored in their beliefs about teaching reading. L and S held multiple belief systems that indicated all three theoretical orientations. Their stated multiple beliefs about reading consistently acted on their beliefs about teaching reading. While LY's stated beliefs about reading were not consistently reflected in her responses about reading instruction, she still indicated dual beliefs in her written responses to both types of questions. Her beliefs about reading showed the cognitivist and constructivist orientations, whereas her beliefs about teaching reading were behaviorist and constructivist. Finally, X and R both held mixed reading beliefs that consisted of both behaviorist and constructivist orientations. Those mixed reading beliefs were consistently reflected in their stated responses to both reading and reading teaching questions.

All in all, findings of the written survey responses indicated dual, multiple, and mixed beliefs about reading and reading instruction across all four cases.

TABLE 13   Qualitative analysis data on stated beliefs and actual practices

Case	Participant	Age	Gender	Reading beliefs		Teaching beliefs		Actual practice	
				Type	TO	Type	TO	Type	TO
1	Y	28	M	Dual	Beh Cog	Dual	Beh Cog	Dual	Beh Cog
	D	34	F	Dual	Beh Cog	Dual	Beh Cog	Dual	Beh Cog
2	S[a]	48	M	Multiple	Beh(C) Cog(C) Con(P)	Multiple	Beh(C) Cog(C) Con(P)	Dual	Beh Con
	L	34	F	Multiple	Beh Cog(C) Con	Multiple	Beh Cog(C) Con	Dual	Beh Con
3	LY[a]	38	F	Dual	Cog Con(C)	Dual	Beh(P) Con(C)	Multiple	Beh Cog(C) Con
4	X[a]	44	F	Dual	Cog Con	Dual	Cog Con	Multiple	Beh Cog Con
	R	45	F	Dual	Cog(P) Con(C)	Dual	Cog(P) Con(C)	Multiple	Beh Cog Con

Notes: TO: theoretical orientations.
  All theoretical orientations are abbreviated to the first three letters
  C: core beliefs; P: peripheral beliefs
  a   teacher team leader

Instead of holding a dominant, single belief system, all teachers held at least two types of beliefs in their stated responses.

The second key similarity between the teachers within the case studies was that they all indicated cognitivist reading beliefs. In contrast with the quantitative findings – in which the 96 teachers in their stated responses expressed behaviorist reading beliefs more often than the other two reading beliefs – teachers in the selected cases all exhibited cognitivist paradigms in their stated beliefs about reading and reading teaching.

Some of the selected participants in fact held core cognitivist beliefs. For example, while L and S held multiple belief systems that included all three theoretical orientations, they both regarded the cognitivist beliefs as most important. In contrast, the other teachers also held cognitivist beliefs, but they viewed them as peripheral. Regardless, all of the qualitative participants uniformly held cognitivist beliefs in their stated belief systems. Cognitivist beliefs that focused on comprehension or understanding of certain text concepts, cultural knowledge, and reading skills were reflected in each of their stated responses to varying degrees.

Finally, all teachers provided evidence for consistency in their theoretical orientations between reading beliefs and reading teaching beliefs. In Cases 1, 3, and 4, teachers held dual belief systems, whereas S & L in Case 2 held multiple-belief systems (see Table 13).

In addition, in most cases, this consistency carried over into their classification of core or peripheral beliefs. For example, behaviorist and cognitivist perspectives were core beliefs in S's stated responses about defining reading, while constructivist beliefs were relatively peripheral. That core-and-peripheral relationship was transferred to S's stated beliefs about teaching reading. R is another example. Her belief system was built on cognitivist and constructivist orientations – in which the former was peripheral, and the latter was core. This was indicated in both her stated beliefs about reading and her responses about teaching reading.

Differences. Differences between cases in terms of teachers' beliefs about reading and reading instruction were also indicated. First, while most participants in the qualitative part made connections between how they perceived reading and how they believed that reading instruction should be taught, there was still an exceptional case (LY) in which a teacher contradicted her beliefs about reading and teaching reading. Instead of the multiple belief system shown in her reading beliefs, she displayed a dual belief system in her stated beliefs about teaching reading. As for the other three cases, regardless of the number and categories of theoretical orientations in their stated beliefs about reading and teaching reading, they indicated a consistency between the two belief systems.

In addition, as had been reported in the quantitative findings, teachers held different, mixed beliefs. Specifically, teachers across all four cases differed from each case in terms of their belief systems and theoretical orientations. For example, S and Y in Case 2 held a multiple belief system including all three theoretical orientations, whereas Y and D in Case 1 held a dual belief system which included behaviorist and cognitivist theoretical orientations. The qualitative cross-case analysis confirmed this quantitative finding.

4.2   *Actual Practices: Similarities vs. Differences*

Unlike the similarities and differences reflected in stated beliefs, which were mostly classified by theoretical orientations, similarities and differences in actual practices were primarily analyzed in terms of the instructional methods used, which embodied different theories.

Similarities. Classroom observation indicated similarities among case groups, especially for teachers who taught in a behaviorist orientation. First, all teachers' instruction used behaviorist methods, although not all teachers regarded the behaviorist orientation as their core orientation (see Table 13). Case 1 used more decoding methods than the other teachers. These teachers taught reading primarily as an analysis of words and phrases. Typical teaching methods expressed in their stated teaching beliefs included direct/rote instruction, translation, decoding, word-formation rules, a focus-on-form approach, etc. Similarly, Case 2 also used phonics or decoding methods in actual practices. While other groups used fewer behaviorist methods than they did other methods in either cognitivist or constructivist orientation, they all used behaviorist methods in their actual practice.

Second, within the broad scope of behaviorist instruction, teachers frequently used similar instructional methods, including reading aloud, translation, word dictation, and sentence-making. All these were consistent with decoding and behaviorist orientations. For example, both Y and D used word-formation methods in their instruction. L and X, though not in the same group, both used word dictation as a way to evaluate vocabulary comprehension among students. LY and R used pattern drill practice and sentence-making activities in their instruction.

The similarity between methods used by different teachers in different cases was only true for methods falling under the behaviorist umbrella. For example, the instructional methods based on a constructivist orientation led teachers to design different activities with multimodal mediators involved. Generally, methods in the constructivist orientation were more diversified and flexible than the behaviorist methods. The cognitivist orientation, being focused on individual differences, was also less likely to lead to similar classroom practices.

Third, multiple theoretical orientations were reflected in teachers' actual practices. Apart from the finding that all teachers used behaviorist methods in their actual practices, another similarity was that they all used methods representing dual or multiple orientations, instead of a single, dominant orientation in their classroom instruction. For example, LY, X, and R all had a multiple-belief system guiding their actual practice. That is, the behaviorist, cognitivist, and constructivist orientations were all reflected in their classroom instruction. Teachers in Cases 1 and 2 all held dual belief systems informing their classroom instruction. However, the expressed core and peripheral beliefs differed, and each of the paradigms were adopted at different frequencies by the observed teachers (see Table 13). For example, though they all held dual beliefs,

Y and D showed behaviorist and cognitivist beliefs in their actual teaching, whereas L and S held behaviorist and constructivist beliefs in their instruction.

Differences. Classroom observations also indicated differences in teachers' actual practices across the cases. Those differences were analyzed from three perspectives: instructional focus, classroom interaction, and instructional content.

Instructional focus. Teachers in the behaviorist reading orientation tended to provide students with rote instruction, which is typically test-based. the College English Test (CET) is the largest national English-language test in China. It tests students' English-language proficiency. Because CET is a required test for most universities, it may explain why the participants in this study taught test-taking skills in their classes. Five methods frequently utilized during their lessons included reading aloud, pattern drill practice, translation, dictation, and sentence-making. Some teachers, e.g., R and Y, specifically emphasized test-taking skills in their actual practice. R, X, and Y spent approximately 15 to 20 minutes teaching students how to choose correct answers from multiple-choice options or how to guess the meaning of unknown words in context. They also taught students specific vocabulary from the test word list in class. In a typical test-based classroom, rote instruction with few activities or tasks is the predominant method. Students take their notes quietly while their teachers instruct. In behaviorist classes with a test-taking emphasis, minimal peer discussion or feedback was observed.

In contrast to teachers with a behaviorist reading orientation, teachers with a cognitivist reading orientation tended to use methods like close or text structure analysis in their classrooms. As a cognitivist reading orientation focuses on comprehension, teachers would often check students' understanding of every individual sentence or phrase. Also, as a cognitivist reading orientation focuses on the whole text, teachers with this orientation seemed to ask students to see the overall structure of the text first and then move down to understand detailed words or phrases. Also, teachers were observed frequently checking students' understanding of the words, sentences, or texts while providing regular feedback.

In contrast to behaviorist and cognitivist reading orientations, teachers in the constructivist orientation used more tasks than rote instruction. For example, when teaching a new lesson about personalities, X started the lesson with a warm-up activity asking students about their ideal traits in a romantic partner. Instead of directly teaching the vocabulary, X used guiding activities as a means to encourage students to think about the words used to describe a person's qualities. Y asked her students to pair with each other and talk about their real-life experiences to understand a specific concept. By doing so, she guided the students to construct meanings of specific concepts. Through these observations, it became clear that in constructivist classrooms, task-based instruction as the primary means of understanding text or concept meanings was often used.

In sum, a continuum of tasks and teacher-student interactions among the classrooms based on three different reading orientations were indicated, with no orientation emerging as the clear dominating methodology. In terms of the task types and interaction frequencies, in classrooms based on the behaviorist reading orientation, teachers conducted few tasks or activities and seldom interacted directly with students. The most frequently used tasks in this type of classroom were translation and sentence-making activities. This kind of classroom stands on one extreme of the continuum. Then, in the middle of the continuum are the classrooms based on the cognitivist reading orientation. This orientation equipped teachers with relatively more tasks and more feedback for the students. At the opposite end of the continuum stands the constructivism-based classroom, where teaching is primarily task-based, and interactions among students and teachers are key.

Classroom interaction. Similar to the task continuum, there was a continuum of teacher-student interactions among the classrooms based on the three different reading orientations. The way teachers interacted with students seemed to indicate which theoretical orientations they believed in.

For example, some teachers (e.g., Y and D) had more interactions with their students. Classroom observations indicated that Y and D interacted with students on a regular basis in their classes. Their interaction was often used as a means to check whether students had understood a certain word or concept. This focus on understanding or comprehension of a certain concept indicated a cognitivist orientation.

LY did not interact with students as frequently as Y and D did. However, the way she interacted with students was identical to the style used by Y and D – she used interaction to check students' understanding of a certain word or concept.

Conversely, S and R seldom interacted with students in their classes, instead of using direct or rote instruction in class. L and X also did not interact with students very often but left time for students to do class activities. Classroom observations yielded the finding that teachers who used less interaction and more rote instruction indicated their stated beliefs to be in the behaviorist orientation. In contrast, teachers who left more time for student activities indicated the constructivist orientation.

Teaching content. Classroom observation indicated differences among the selected groups in the content they preferred to teach in their classes. For example, linguistic knowledge like grammar, vocabulary, and text structure was often taught in behaviorist classroom environments. Pragmatic or language-association knowledge, such as background knowledge, cultural content, or association with real-world problems, indicated the cognitivist and constructivist orientations.

Classroom observations indicated many differences between the various teachers with regards to their content focus and theoretical orientations in the classroom. For example, D taught vocabulary and grammar that related to language knowledge and competence. Both Y and D taught smaller linguistic units, such as grammar, words, and sentence structures, which indicated a behaviorist orientation. In addition, these behaviorist language teachers believed in repeating and rephrasing what students have learned, and they often asked students to repeat sentences aloud. Language learning in this orientation seemed to be mechanical and closely associated with repetition and association.

In contrast, LY and S focused on teaching the background or cultural knowledge of a text and designed activities through which students internalized their learning of the text. This was related to language performance, which highlights the importance of constructing meaning through activities. As cognitivist and constructivist practitioners, those teachers stated beliefs that learning is a change in individuals' mental structures, enabling them to show changes in behavior. Their focus was on what is in the learner's head, coupled with the student's behavior. Therefore, their instructional methods were typically focused on the association between knowledge learning and the knowledge learned. Triggers were used to activate what their students had learned and combined the learned knowledge with the text they were required to read in class. For example, cultural books were frequently used by cognitivist-oriented teachers. The teachers' instruction focused on language association instead of language itself.

5   Conceptualization of the Coadaptive and Self-organizing Subsystems

As discussed earlier, the states of the three different subsystems are not stable but instead comprised of a continuum of states with all the three subsystems moving between the two ends. One end of the continuum is the ideal state when all the three subsystems overlap, and the other end of the continuum is the state when all the three subsystems stand individually and do not overlap any of the other two. Different situations comprise a quadrat (see Figure 11). Specifically, in the top-left picture, the three subsystems, including the reading belief system, the teaching belief system, and the actual practice system, move individually at first, with a tendency to move interactively toward each other.

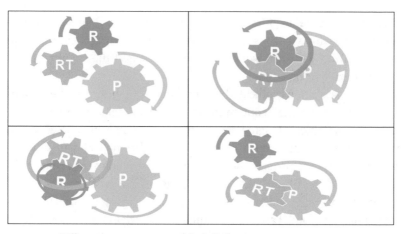

FIGURE 11   Different emergent states of the belief-practice system

If interactions among the three subsystems occur at a relatively similar pace and direction, they may develop an emergent state as in the top-right picture.

However, there are situations, which much more often occur in the real settings, that two of the subsystems move and interact at a relatively similar pace and direction, but the other subsystem of the three moves either faster or slower than the two subsystems. For example, the reading belief system and the teaching belief system move toward each other at a relatively similar pace, either faster or slower than that of the practice system. In addition, the practice system moves fairly straightforward, without an ostension to the other two systems. This kind of exemplar situation may be best presented in the bottom-left picture. Similarly, the bottom-right picture may represent a situation when teaching beliefs and actual practice are consistent. However, the consistency does not show in the reading beliefs. It is worth mentioning that the quadrat may represent most, but not all, of the situations when interactions and coadaptations of different subsystems attempt to make, and these interactions and coadaptations render different emergent states to the whole system. It is also worth mentioning that the quadrat serves as a dynamic representation of the seven specific states and three types of states as depicted in the conceptual nexus of the belief-practice system in Figure 6.

6   Conclusion

In this chapter, I summarized and described the inconsistencies of belief and practice among the seven teachers who were selected and observed in their classrooms. Among them, only two, Y and D, practiced the same orientation in the classroom that they had identified in the survey. Other teachers exhibited some inconsistencies between their stated beliefs and actual practices.

In this chapter, I also provided a conceptualized model on the nexus of different constructs in the book and the coadaptive and dynamic evolution of the three subsystems, including the reading belief system, the teaching belief system, and the actual practice system. I also discussed possible factors that inform or impede the development of the belief-practice system. It is worth arguing that the depiction and proposal of the model draw upon empirical findings of the current study as well as conceptual hypotheses from the existing literature. It is strongly recommended that future works provide further evaluation and adaptation for the model. However, the model does contribute to the existing literature by mapping out different constructs, dynamics, and agents which interact with each other to inform either in theoretical orientations to reading and teaching reading or in actual practice.

References

Anderson, R. C., & Pearson, P. D. (1984). A schema-theoretic view of basic processes in reading. In P. D. Pearson (Ed.), *Handbook of reading research* (pp. 255–291). Longman.

Borg, S. (2003). Teacher cognition in language teaching: A review of research into what language teachers think, know, believe and do. *Language Teaching, 36*(2), 81–109.

Borg, S. (2006). *Teacher cognition and language education: Research and practice.* Continuum.

Borg, S. (2009). English language teachers' conceptions of research. *Applied Linguistics, 30*(3), 355–388.

DeFord, D. (1978). *A validation study of an instrument to determine teachers' theoretical orientation to reading instruction* [PhD dissertation]. Indiana University.

Dörnyei, Z. (2007). Creating a motivating classroom environment. In J. Cummins & C. Davison (Eds.), *International handbook of English language teaching* (Vol. 2, pp. 719–731). Springer.

Ertmer, P. A., & Newby, T. J. (2013). Behaviorism, cognitivism, constructivism: Comparing critical features from an instructional design perspective. *Performance Improvement Quarterly, 26*(2), 43–71.

Goodman, K. (1967). Reading: A psycholinguistic guessing game. *Journal of the Reading Specialist, 6*(4), 126–135.

Goodman, K. (1986). *What's whole in whole language?* Heinemann Educational Books.

Gough, P. B. (1972). Theoretical models and processes of reading. In J. F. Kavanagh & I. G. Mattingly (Eds.), *Language by ear and by eye* (pp. 661–685). MIT Press.

Gough, P. B. (1993). The beginning of decoding. *Reading and Writing: An Interdisciplinary Journal, 5*(2), 181–192.

LaBerge, D., & Samuels, S. (1974). Toward a theory of automatic information processing in reading. *Cognitivist Psychology, 6*(2), 293–323.

Lantolf, J. P. (Ed.). (2000). *Sociocultural theory and second language learning.* Oxford University Press.

Morrison, T. G., Wilcox, B., Madrigal, J. L., Roberts, S., & Hintze, E. (1999). Teachers' theoretical orientations toward reading and pupil control ideology: A national survey. *Reading Research and Instruction, 38*(4), 333–350.

Richardson, R., & Kramer, E. H. (2006). Abduction as the type of inference that characterizes the development of a grounded theory. *Qualitative Research, 6*(4), 497–513.

Rosenblatt, L. M. (1994). The transactional theory of reading and writing. In R. B. Ruddell, M. R. Ruddell, & H. Singer (Eds.), *Theoretical models and processes of reading* (4th ed., pp. 1057–1092). International Reading Association.

Rumelhart, D. E. (1980). Schemata: The building blocks of cognition. In R. J. Spiro, B. C. Bruce, & W. F. Brewer (Eds.), *Theoretical issues in reading comprehension* (pp. 33–58). Erlbaum.

Skinner, B. F. (1938). *The behavior of organisms.* Appleton-Century-Crofts.

Smith, F. (1971). *Understanding reading.* Holt, Rinehart & Winston.

Stanovich, K. E. (1980). Toward an interactive-compensatory model of individual differences in the development of reading fluency. *Reading Research Quarterly, 16*(1), 32–71.

Vygotsky, L. S. (1978). *Mind in society: The development of higher psychological processes.* Harvard University Press.

Zainal, Z. (2003). Critical review of reading model and theories in first and second language. *Human Journal/Jurnal Kemanusiaan, 1*(2), 104–124.

CHAPTER 8

Conclusion: A CDST Model to Study Language Teacher Beliefs and Practices

1 Overview of the Chapter

In this chapter, I discuss the findings of the study based on three primary research questions. I provide a review of the research questions and present the key findings under each. I also discuss the implications of the study. In particular, I address teacher education, teacher reflection, and teacher team leaders and suggest what might be done to improve teacher education and faculty professional development programs. I also outline insights gained from the findings in support of my conceptualized, theoretical model to study language teacher beliefs and practices. The model presented here provides the reader with insights for future studies.

Three research questions guided this study. The first question investigated the characteristics of Chinese EFL teachers' stated beliefs about English reading and reading instruction. Findings indicated that complexity was the primary feature of the belief systems. Specifically, three major theoretical orientations (behaviorism, cognitivism, and constructivism) were matrixed with three types of belief systems or subbeliefs (dominant, dual, and multiple). This multilayered matrix made up the belief system complex. Under the complex matrix, the quantitative findings of the study further indicated more complex relationships among beliefs within a specific theoretical orientation and across different orientations. Discussion on only one research question may not provide a holistic picture of the characteristics of the belief system. Therefore, some of these complex relationships within the belief system were explained through discussions on Research Questions 2 and 3.

The second research question investigated whether Chinese EFL teachers' stated beliefs about English reading were consistently indicated in their stated beliefs about teaching reading. On the one hand, quantitative findings from this study indicated that there was a statistically significant association between reading beliefs and teaching beliefs only in the constructivist orientation ($p < .05$). However, the association was not statistically strong ($\phi = .060$, $p < .05$). On the other hand, there was no statistical association between reading beliefs and teaching beliefs in either behaviorist or cognitivist orientations.

© KONINKLIJKE BRILL NV, LEIDEN, 2022 | DOI: 10.1163/9789004506541_008

The inconsistent, nonlinear relationships between reading beliefs and reading teaching beliefs made the belief system even more complex.

The third question investigated whether Chinese EFL teachers' beliefs about reading and teaching reading were consistently indicated in their actual practices in the classroom. Findings from both within- and cross-case studies in the qualitative part indicated that both consistencies and inconsistencies existed between teachers' stated beliefs and their actual practices. For example, only two participants, in my observations, practiced the same orientations in the classroom that they had identified in the survey, but many participants had areas of overlap. Findings of the discrepancies within different cases yielded a complex, nonlinear relationship between beliefs and practice. Discussions on the three research questions also worked as a whole to describe and explain the complex, nonlinear, and unpredictable characteristics of the belief system.

2 Characteristics of Chinese EFL Teachers' Stated Beliefs about English Reading and Teaching Reading

Regarding Research Question 1, findings indicated that multiple reading orientations coexisted in these Chinese EFL teachers' belief systems. As explained in Chapter 4, a dominant reading belief system represents only one theoretical orientation. A dual belief system stands for the mixture of two theoretical orientations to reading. A matrix with the three potential pairs of dual theoretical orientations was indicated in the study: behaviorism and cognitivism (1 & 2); cognitivism and constructivism (2 & 3); and behaviorism and constructivism (1 & 3). A multiple beliefs system includes all three theoretical orientations.

In this study, most of the teacher participants, instead of holding a single, unique orientation, embraced multiple and diverse reading and teaching orientations. Multiple orientations made the belief system complex. Quantitative findings indicated that irrespective of reading beliefs or reading teaching beliefs, any orientation was different from the others in its percentage. There was not an even distribution among the three reading belief systems or theoretical orientations. For example, teachers with a dominant, constructivist reading orientation accounted for only 3.9%, whereas teachers holding a dominant, behaviorist reading orientation (the most common in the study) accounted for only 18.1%. Another example is teachers holding a dual reading belief system accounted for 38.8 % of the whole sample for reading beliefs, whereas teachers holding a multiple reading belief system accounted for only 11.1%.

Likewise, qualitative findings indicated that teachers in different cases held different reading and teaching belief systems. In this study, teachers Y, D, X,

R, and LY all held a dual belief system, whereas S and L held a multiple belief system. Each system may consist of different orientations leading to different beliefs. This finding is consistent with findings from previous studies. For example, in a case study of comparing beliefs and practices between a novice and an experienced ESL teacher, Farrell and Bennis (2013) showed the complexity of teacher belief systems and stated that "teachers may have many competing beliefs in play at any one time" (p. 163). Zheng (2013) also found the coexistence of different types of beliefs made the belief system complex.

In addition to the complex coexistence of different theoretical orientations, the findings of the study indicated that relationships among different beliefs were nonlinear and unpredictable. Specifically, two kinds of unpredictabilities occurred in the study. The first unpredictability occurred in belief systems. Specifically, the occurrence of a specific belief system in the stated beliefs did not necessarily indicate its occurrence in the actual practice. For example, S and L were advocates of multiple reading beliefs in their survey responses but then practitioners of a dual belief system in their actual practices. The second unpredictability occurred in theoretical orientations. Specifically, statistical percentages of a certain belief system did not necessarily indicate similar percentages of the belief system in teaching and vice versa. For example, the largest percentage in reading beliefs was the dual belief system (38.8%), whereas the largest percentage in reading teaching beliefs was the single, behaviorist belief system (37.8%).

Likewise, qualitative findings indicated that having one orientation in reading and teaching beliefs was not a significant predictor of which orientation the teacher might hold in actual practice. For example, both S and L held cognitivist reading and teaching beliefs in their survey responses. However, they did not indicate the cognitivist orientation in their actual practices.

The nonlinear, unpredictable relationship then made the participants' teacher belief systems even more complex. This finding was similar to study findings regarding teachers' stated beliefs about teaching reading (Pajares, 1992; Phipps & Borg, 2009; Skott, 2001). In Chapter 5, I offered hypothetical, empirical, and theoretical explanations for this complex phenomenon.

3 Teachers' Stated Beliefs about English Reading and Teaching Reading

With respect to Research Question 2, the quantitative findings indicated that there was no significant association between reading beliefs and teaching beliefs in teachers holding behaviorist or cognitivist theoretical orientations.

This again confirmed the unpredictable feature of the beliefs system. As evidenced by their survey responses, while many teachers held behaviorist or cognitivist reading beliefs, they may not necessarily hold the same level of behaviorist or cognitivist teaching beliefs.

While the quantitative findings did not indicate any association between reading beliefs and teaching beliefs in the behaviorist and cognitivist orientations, the qualitative data in the study indicated something different: how teachers defined reading was largely consistent with how they defined teaching reading. Specifically, except for LY, the six other teachers indicated consistencies between their stated beliefs about reading and stated beliefs about teaching reading. One of the possible explanations for the inconsistency between the quantitative findings and the qualitative findings is the sampling methods. Through introducing different strategies for purposeful sampling, Patton (2002) explained that the aim of purposeful sampling methods is "to capture *major variations* rather than to identify *a common core*" (p. 40). Through the purposeful sampling method, there may be a chance that all participants selected in the qualitative part indicated coincidentally different results from the whole sample of the study.

The consistency between beliefs about reading and those about teaching reading in the qualitative part illuminated the following subfindings. First, through analyzing the seven participants' stated beliefs, I found that multiple beliefs instead of single, dominant beliefs existed in their belief systems. Specifically, none of the seven participants in the study held a single, dominant theoretical orientation. Five of the teachers held a dual belief system, and the other two (i.e., S and L) held a multiple belief system. This finding reconfirmed what had been discussed in Research Question 1.

Second, all seven teachers held cognitivist teaching beliefs, but not all the teachers held behaviorist or constructivist beliefs. This finding was interesting but contradictory to what had been indicated in the quantitative results. As discussed earlier, teachers exhibited more behaviorist and constructivist beliefs than cognitive beliefs in the survey responses. One reasonable explanation is that behaviorist beliefs were the earliest and oldest beliefs and therefore considered to be deep-rooted and difficult to alter (Borg, 2003, 2011; Gutierrez Almarza, 1996; Johnson, 1992). Constructivist beliefs were then, as discussed, the latest beliefs that guided innovation in reading instruction, and thus may be more frequently used than the cognitivist beliefs (Johnson, 1992; Kırkgöz, 2008). However, while quantitative results indicated both the earliest and the latest theoretical orientations and had yielded more teacher beliefs than the cognitivist orientation, the qualitative findings indicated that all seven teachers believed in the cognitivist orientation, the orientation that focuses on student reading comprehension.

Third, a major finding in this study indicated that the seven teachers were able to apply what they defined as core or peripheral beliefs about reading to their core or peripheral beliefs about teaching reading. This finding confirmed findings of the previous studies. For example, Phipps and Borg (2009), by investigating tensions between grammar teaching beliefs and actual practices of three teachers, hypothesized that core beliefs were more stable and influential than peripheral beliefs in shaping teachers' instructional decisions. In this study, the theoretical orientation that indicated a teacher's core beliefs about reading was in most cases the same theoretical orientation that indicated their core beliefs about teaching reading. This finding was also consistent with the theoretical orientation in teachers' peripheral beliefs; it again showed that teachers' stated beliefs about reading were consistent with their stated beliefs about teaching reading in the study.

4   Teachers' Stated Beliefs and Actual Practices

With respect to Research Question 3, findings from both within-case studies and cross-case studies indicated that teachers' stated beliefs about teaching reading were both consistently and inconsistently indicated in their actual practices.

This finding from within-case studies confirmed findings from previous studies in two different camps. Some of these indicated that stated beliefs affect teachers' actual practices in the classroom (Farrell & Kun, 2007; Golombek, 1998; Johnson, 1994; Ng & Farrell, 2003). However, other empirical studies indicated inconsistencies between stated beliefs and actual practices (Basturkmen et al., 2004; Farrell & Kun, 2007; Feryok, 2008; Orafi & Borg, 2009; Phipps & Borg, 2009; Chai et al., 2009). The within-case studies of the whole study yielded similar findings of the previous studies. Specifically, Y and D were the two teachers and the only case that showed consistencies between their stated beliefs about reading and their stated beliefs about teaching reading. They also held consistent theoretical orientations in their actual practices. In contrast, the three other cases with five teachers showed inconsistencies in either their beliefs about reading and teaching reading or their beliefs and practices. Some teachers (e.g., S and L) held more types of theoretical orientations in their stated beliefs than in their actual practices. Some others (e.g., LY, X, and R) held fewer theoretical orientations in their stated beliefs than in their actual practices. This study joined the existing literature by confirming that while consistency existed between stated beliefs and actual practices among all teachers, inconsistencies were more frequent. The nonconsensual results between consistencies and inconsistencies reconfirmed the complexity of the belief system and confirmed the nonlinear, interactive nature of the relationship between beliefs and practices.

Apart from the findings from within-case studies, cross-case studies also yielded consistencies and inconsistencies between stated beliefs and actual practices. First, this study confirmed that teachers' specific theoretical orientations highly influenced their selection of instructional methods. Specifically, teachers who reported the instructional strategies under a specific theoretical orientation in their stated teaching beliefs may transfer the reported strategies in their actual practices. This is one consistency between teachers' beliefs and practices, particularly for the behaviorist theoretical orientation. For example, teachers in a behaviorist reading orientation gave students more test-based, rote instruction. Five specific methods were used frequently during their lessons. These methods included reading aloud, pattern drill practice, translation, dictation, and sentence-making. Some teachers, e.g., R and Y, emphasized test-taking skills in their actual practice. Teachers with a cognitive reading orientation used methods like cloze or text structure analysis in their classrooms. In contrast to the behaviorist and cognitivist reading orientations, teachers in the constructivist orientation used more time for student peer discussion than that for rote instruction.

A variety of possible explanations may be given for how theoretical orientations influence the selection and use of instructional methods. These explanations centered around how "epistemological beliefs play a key role in knowledge interpretation and cognitive monitoring" (Pajares, 1992). The centrality of epistemological beliefs, which concern the certainty, process, and nature of knowledge, has been confirmed in previous studies (Anderson, 1985; Kitchener, 1986; Nespor, 1987; Nisbett & Ross, 1980; Peterman, 1991; Posner et al., 1982). In this study, teachers' different orientations were based on their different epistemological beliefs, as confirmed by the previous studies. These different epistemological beliefs then influenced the selection of different instructional methods.

However, there were also inconsistencies indicated from the cross-case analysis. For example, one major finding from the qualitative part was that all seven observed teachers held a behaviorist orientation in their actual practices, as they all used behaviorist methods in these practices. This finding indicated inconsistency with the unanimous theoretical orientation suggested by their stated beliefs. As discussed earlier, all seven teachers held the cognitivist orientation in their stated beliefs about reading and teaching reading. However, when observed teaching in the classroom, their practice did not indicate that they all used cognitivist instructional methods. This finding indicated that teachers' theoretical orientations in actual practice were not necessarily consistent with those theoretical orientations shown in their stated beliefs and vice versa. In other words, having a specific orientation in stated beliefs was not a significant predictor of holding this orientation in actual practice.

5   Theoretical Implication: A CDST Model on EFL Teacher Beliefs and Practice

In this chapter, I provide a conceptualized model (Garner & Kaplan, 2019) on studying reading teachers' beliefs and practice in an EFL context from a CDST perspective. The model helps explain the nexus of different constructs in the book and especially how the belief system of the reading teachers interacts and coadapts with their actual practice. Illustrations and explanations of subsections of the whole model are presented as well. Key concepts and tenets in CDST and their connections with the model and sections are also elaborated on throughout the chapter.

Approaches to propose a model in CDST may diverge: some approaches attempt to draw quantitative and mathematical models in a positivist paradigm. These sampled modeling methods may include dynamic systems modeling, computational modeling, agent-based modeling, and network modeling (Richardson et al., 2014). All these models have different advantages and disadvantages, which overlap or compensate for each other in one way or another. However, all these modeling methods are profoundly rooted or widely used in mathematical or psychological studies that attempt to simulate how a complex system runs. While helpful and insightful, these modeling methods cannot fit into the current study. First, different paradigms guiding these modeling methods may not fit the current pragmatist paradigm in the study. Second, the highly simulation-based modeling methods may better map out relationships among different constructs in a short-term, relatively fixed setting than in a long-term, dynamic, and scalar context (Steenbeek & van Geert, 2013). Last but not least, choosing a modeling method that fits the current study field and its audience is more important than drawing fancy but sophisticated models beyond my expertise.

Therefore, I depict and propose the model in an interpretivist rather than a positivist approach. Mapping out the relationships among these studied constructs was thus not totally statistically guided but instead followed a meta-theoretical, conceptualized approach (Overton, 2013). Similar conceptualized approaches have been adopted in previous studies (e.g., Kaplan & Garner, 2017, 2018; Li & Ren, 2020; Zheng, 2015). An interpretivist approach requires sound

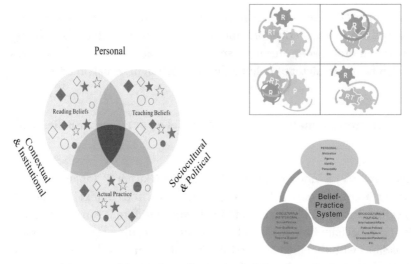

Personal

FIGURE 12   A CDST model to study reading teacher beliefs and practice in an EFL context

logic and effective argumentative analyses. I thus refer to a Venn diagram in logic to set up the base for the model. Therefore, based on the findings in the previous chapters, especially in Chapters 4, 5, and 6, I propose the following model (see Figure 12).

The model is actually comprised of three different informative sets, including a map presenting the nexus of the belief-practice system, a quadrat describing the dynamic process of three different subsystems, and a cyclical loop representing different factors informing or restricting the development of the belief-practice system. Each set serves a certain function to explain the system and works with the other sets to form a holistic model. In the following sections, I will analyze and explain different sets. A good application of CDST includes an extensive discussion on the constructs, agents, components,

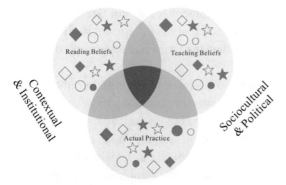

Personal

FIGURE 13
The conceptual nexus of reading teachers' beliefs and practices in an EFL context

and their interactions among the system (Larsen-Freeman & Cameron, 2008). In this section, I attempt to present how this model meets the criteria of the application as such.

5.1   *Nexus of the Belief-Practice System for Reading Teachers*
The belief-practice system includes three subsystems, i.e., the reading belief system, the reading teaching belief system, and the actual practice system, which interact with each other. The two belief subsystems comprised of stated or professed beliefs about reading and teaching reading and contributed to the whole belief system. It is worth mentioning that some previous studies (e.g., Zheng, 2015) regarded teachers' actual practices as an embedded construct in the whole belief system. In my study, I listed it as an individual but coadaptive system that is identical to the two belief systems. The three subsystems together contributed to a holistic, belief-practice system. I drew upon Steenbeek and van Geert (2013), which studied the learning-teaching trajectory from the CDST perspective and argued the two systems (beliefs vs. practices) coadapt and evolve with each other in a scalar way in the current study. Beliefs and practices are also viewed as a trajectory, as we teachers believe what we learn and then teach what we believe. Our learning comprises our content-area knowledge and pedagogical knowledge, which contribute to our repertoire and form our beliefs. Then, our beliefs guide us to teach and practice in real settings. In this study, reading beliefs inform reading teaching beliefs and then inform teachers' actual practices in their classrooms. The three identical subsystems coexist in a dynamic way instead of in any hierarchical order. In addition, my background as a Chinese person has provided me with a philosophical, Chinese perspective that belief and practice should stand in harmony as a holism (*zhi xing he yi*), no matter whether the two compete with or assimilate each other within the holism. Therefore, I term the model as a belief-practice system instead of simply as a belief system.

The core of the model is a Venn diagram with three circles interlocked or partially overlapped. The three circles represent the three subsystems, including beliefs about reading, teaching reading, and actual practices. The linked sections represent different trajectories that the three subsystems run or operate, and they contribute to seven specific, different states, the sample of which are listed in Figure 14.

The first sample state (see Figure 14), which is located in the far-left end of the sampled states, is the focal point and the core of the Venn diagram. It represents all three subsystems consistently and identically develops at the same rate and in the same direction. Specifically, an EFL teacher's beliefs about reading are consistently revealed through the teacher's beliefs about teaching

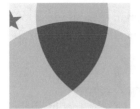

FIGURE 14   Sampled states of coadaptive subsystems

reading. The consistency between reading beliefs and teaching beliefs then informs the teacher's actual practices in the classroom, guiding the teacher to make any classroom decisions and facilitate the instruction. For example, two of the teachers, Y and D, in the previous chapters held dual theoretical orientations to both reading beliefs and teaching beliefs, and they taught as they planned and believed in the actual classrooms.

The first state is an ideal state when all the three subsystems coevolve and develop at the same rate (see Figure 15). However, an ideal state does not equal the best state. It may not be safe to conclude a linear relationship between beliefs and practices indicates a good thing. As teachers, we learn, develop, and grow to be effective instructors when we meet with difficulties and challenges in our classrooms; some of the difficulties and challenges may come from inconsistency between our beliefs and the practices. With this premise, it might be dangerous to conclude the first state is the attractor state. It may be an attractor state for those teachers who argue consistency between beliefs and practices is necessary; however, it is definitely not the attractor state for those teachers who like taking risks and learn from inconsistency between beliefs and practices.

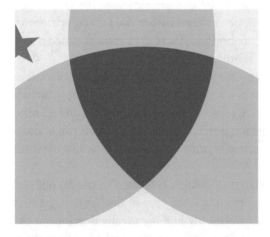

FIGURE 15
Sampled states of coadaptive
subsystems

FIGURE 16
Sampled states of coadaptive subsystems

Another type of sampled state is a rare state when only two of the three systems converge in their orientations (see the middle image in Figure 14). In other words, only two of the subsystems are consistent in their orientations, and the last subsystem among the three is different from the other two subsystems. There are three sampled states, including states 2, 3, and 4 (shown in Figure 14). Specifically, beliefs of reading orientations and teaching reading in identical orientations may converge; however, the consistent belief system may not be shown through the actual practice. In other words, while teachers believe how reading is defined will inform their beliefs about teaching reading, they may meet with challenges in the actual classroom that impede their input of the beliefs in their practice. Another exemplar situation is when teachers believed in certain orientations in their reading beliefs but act differently in their actual practice, which has been informed by their teaching beliefs. In other words, while their teaching beliefs are consistently revealed through their actual practice, these teaching beliefs are not consistent with their reading beliefs. The last exemplar state is one in which reading beliefs are consistently revealed through actual practice. These reading beliefs are inconsistent with the teaching beliefs held by teachers.

For example, in the study, both S and L held multiple orientations in their reading and reading teaching beliefs; however, they taught in a dual-orientation approach. Similarly, LY, R, and X held a dual-orientation belief system. Despite their reading or teaching beliefs, they taught in a multiple-orientation approach. In the exemplar state reading beliefs are consistently revealed through actual practice – reading beliefs that are inconsistent with the teaching beliefs held by teachers. This state is not typically found in the current study.

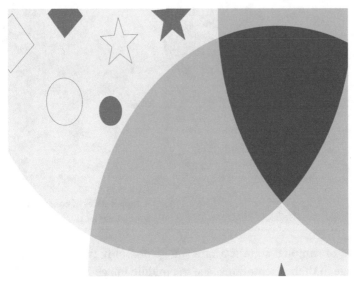

FIGURE 17   Sampled states of coadaptive subsystems

The last type of state is the state when three subsystems share three pairs of dual but not triple consistencies in theoretical orientations. In other words, every two subsystems among the three are identical in their orientations; however, there is no consistency across the three subsystems as a whole. Three states as such are listed in Figure 17. Specifically, there might be situations in theory that teachers hold a dual-orientation beliefs system that differs from the dual orientations in their actual practice. For example, a teacher may hold both behaviorist and cognitivist orientations in their belief systems but then may teach in the way that cognitivist and constructivist approaches are frequently adopted in their actual practice. Another example might be when teachers hold both behaviorist and cognitivist orientations in their belief systems but then may teach in the way that behaviorist and constructivist approaches are frequently adopted in their actual practice. I don't play mathematical probability here but may use these examples to help map out a matrix of the possible dual consistencies in mind.

The key feature of the state is there is *at least* one identical orientation between any two of the three states. With these hypothetical and theoretical arguments, I found a couple of empirical examples in the current study based on the findings in the previous chapters. For example, LY in the study held a dual-orientation reading system, with both cognitivist and constructivist orientations in the system; she also held a dual-orientation teaching system, with both behaviorist and constructivist orientations in the system; she held a multiple-orientation practice system, with behaviorist, cognitivist, and

constructivist orientations in the system. It is shown that a cognitivist orientation was in place across all the three subsystems.

It is worth mentioning that the three types of states, as well as the seven
individual states, are not constant. They may represent a dynamic continuum
of states with all the specific states and types of states moving in-between. The
CDST argues that subsystems are coadaptive and dynamic, bringing about any
chances that provoke new, emergent behaviors (Steenbeek & van Geert, 2013;
Zheng, 2015). The initial state might be the three subsystems that stand alone
and then begin their interactions to move across the other states. However, in
the study, it might not be safe to define any initial state or attractor state, as
each individual teacher may have different initial states and attractor states.
As discussed earlier, an ideal state does not equal the best state or the attractor
state. It may not be safe to conclude that a linear relationship between beliefs
and practices indicates a good thing. An attractor state for those teachers who
argue consistency between beliefs and practices is necessary may not be the
attractor state for those teachers who like taking risks and learn from inconsistency between beliefs and practices. However, the initial state does determine
the attractor state or interactions these subsystems may make during the complex, dynamic, and systemic process.

5.2   *Cyclical Loop of Informative Factors in the Belief-Practice System*

As one of the important parts of the model, I argue that essential factors may
inform or impede the development of the belief-practice system. While my
data analysis and findings in the previous chapters of the study can only offer
exemplar excerpts to support my argument, I may pave the way for future studies which attempt to extend the line of inquiry. Specifically, three types of factors may be presented: personal, contextual & institutional, and sociocultural
& political factors. They may, to some extent, echo the previous classifications
(e.g., Li & Ren, 2020; Zheng, 2015) in terms of micro-, exo-, and macro-contexts
of factors. They may also resonate with Garner and Kaplan (2018) in terms of
social context, culture, domain, dispositions, and emotion. While classifications of these factors diverge in these works and the current study, the primary
types of factors may converge in one way or another. The three types of major
factors comprise a cyclical loop of the belief-practice system (see Figure 18).

Functions of these factors are generally twofold: they may cause tensions
between beliefs and practice. In other words, what teachers believe and plan
for their classes may not be consistently presented in their actual practice.
They may also serve as stimuli to ensure consistency between beliefs and practice among the teachers. In other words, they support what teachers believe
and plan prior to the actual practice and facilitate the implementation of these

FIGURE 18   Cyclical loop of factors in the belief-practice system

beliefs and plans in the actual classroom. In the remainder of this section, I elaborate on these three primary types of factors with examples.

Personal factors may include but are not limited to motivation, agency, identity, and personality. They look into teachers' psychological and cognitive constructs and how they perceive the world or help them make plans or decisions for their instructions. For example, a teacher with great motivation and agency may stick strictly to what he or she has planned for the class. They try hard to implement their instructions based on what they have put into the lesson plans. In the current study, for example, Y and D were two exemplar teachers with such motivation and agency. They managed to finish their classes by completing all the planned goals. Reading beliefs, teaching beliefs, and actual practice among those teachers showed relatively stable, consistent relationships.

Contextual and institutional factors may include departmental, school, or institutional policies, peer scaffolding, student acceptance, regional support, etc. All these factors serve as institutional or contextual affordances to teachers. For example, a teacher may plan for a lesson quite well and attempt to teach the plan in a multimodal approach. However, the multimodal approach requires the teacher to purchase necessary teaching kits, devices, or experimental tools at a high cost. These expenses cannot be reimbursed by the department or the school. The dilemma between the planned class and the class to be taught in a real setting may serve as an excellent example of the tension between beliefs and practice. Take the same teacher as an example, but think about another contextual or institutional factor, such as student acceptance. The multimodal approach would require the students to participate or take part in many activities; however, some students who are introverted or shy may not be willing to participate or cooperate. Typically in the Chinese EFL context, students are seen as passive speakers but active listeners (Gao, 2013) and keen to develop their test-taking skills. The degree of student acceptance thus serves as an impeding factor that can cause tensions between beliefs and practice among teachers in the Chinese EFL context.

Sociocultural and political factors may include international affairs, political policies, or force majeure (such as a natural catastrophe or a disaster or even an unexpected pandemic). The best example at this point might be the unexpected, ever-spreading COVID-19. This unexpected pandemic has caused most school experiences to move online (Gao et al., 2021). We, as teachers, may understand how online courses differ from face-to-face courses. Typically, the online resources for designing a curriculum and lessons are not fully available and accessible in the Chinese EFL context. This may cause tensions between what is generally believed to be what teaching is and what is actually taught through online platforms. Another sociocultural or political factor is (inter)national political policy (Gao, 2020). This is typically true for transnational teachers who were educated in one context but taught in another context. For example, a device or certain teaching materials that a teacher believes to be suitable or appropriate resources in one context might not be acceptable in another.

6 Practical Implications for EFL Teachers and Teacher Team Leaders

In closing, I aim to uncover any hidden or missing pieces that I did not address (but should be addressed). These elements might provide further insight into teachers actions and help them improve their practices. Going through my transcriptions of the classroom observations, I noticed an imbalance between teacher talk and student talk in the classroom. This imbalance made me think about what suggestions I could give to teachers involved in the study and beyond. It also made me think about what theory or conceptual framework I could use to provide my reasoning for the suggestions.

One of the primary findings of the current study indicates that there are inconsistencies between teacher beliefs and practices. The findings provide insights for future studies that could be concerned with how these inconsistencies might be caused by factors including experiences and classroom contexts. Learning and teaching do not occur in a vacuum but instead are shaped by the environment and the people involved. This knowledge led me to turn to frameworks that tie in more closely with the human factors affecting beliefs. I used the zone of proximal development (ZPD) as a conceptual framework to discuss this study's implications for teachers and teacher team leaders. At most Chinese universities, teacher team leaders are individuals who are responsible for organizing faculty meetings for teachers and evaluating teachers' practices. In the current study, S, LY, and X were all teacher team leaders.

Vygotsky (1978) defined the ZPD as "the distance between the actual developmental level as determined by independent problem solving and the level of potential development as determined through problem-solving under adult guidance, or in collaboration with more capable peers" (p. 86). He conceptualized the ZPD to explain how a group or paired learning can be more effective when combining certain ability levels than students learning independently. Simply stated, Vygotsky posited that what students can do together today, they can do by themselves tomorrow. This fundamental principle from the ZPD applies to learning at all levels, from college classrooms to teacher-enrichment programs. Based on the transcriptions of classroom observations, I see three major implications for teachers and teacher team leaders to consider.

First, as I mentioned earlier, I noted an imbalance between teacher talk and student talk in some of my classroom transcriptions. Discussion in all classrooms was primarily teacher-led. Specifically, I found that students were given little opportunity to talk, other than answering questions posed by the teacher. When student talk was observed, it mostly took the form of either a quick yes/no response or simple one-word or two-word answers to teacher questions. Student talk typically took the form of responses and answers rather than that of actual dialogue between teacher and student. Vygotsky's developmental theory stresses that learners do not engage in classroom tasks and activities without involving their social relationships, and their psychological processes, including self-regulation, are developed through interactions with people and learning context (Stetsenko & Vianne, 2009). Providing students with more time to talk could increase student engagement in the reading and learning process. Thus, I would suggest that teachers spend time reflecting on the amount and balance of talk that occurs between themselves and their students in their classrooms. Specifically, I suggest that teachers create a classroom environment in which talk between teachers and students is more balanced – or even in which student talk occurs more than teacher talk. More time could also be provided to students for interacting with other students and also for communicating with teachers. If teachers design classroom activities and tasks that require student participation, they could align coherently with what Vygotsky posited: what students will be able to do together today, they will be able to do by themselves tomorrow.

Second, as mentioned earlier, the fundamental principle from the ZPD applies not only to student learning but also to teacher learning. Specifically, just as students would benefit from interaction and communication with their teachers and peers, teachers need the same. Through interaction and communication with peers, teachers may be prompted to reflect on their actual practices, share reflections, and think together about what instructional practices make teaching effective. While it may be abrupt or biased to assume that novice teachers are less capable than experienced teachers in their teaching performance, it is suggested that novice teachers talk more and reflect with experienced teachers (Plehn et al., 1998). Vygotsky's ZPD (1978) highlighted the important and necessary process that a novice learner needs to go through to learn from an expert. Through interaction with peers, teachers can learn from those who have more experience in the field of teaching. Peer talk may help teachers think about how to improve their current teaching and acquire new knowledge. In other words, what teachers are able to do together through discussion today, they will be able to do through practice by themselves tomorrow.

Third, I would like to provide a deeper explanation as to why reflection is not only important to teachers but also to teacher team leaders. The findings of this study indicated that many teachers who believed in cognitivist practice showed no signs of implementing that framework in their classrooms. This has significant implications for teacher team leaders. Teacher team leaders organize faculty meetings for teachers. At these faculty meetings, one of their major responsibilities is to ask teachers to reflect on their teaching from the previous week or month and share these reflections with their team members. Besides offering an opportunity for proximal development, these meetings are also opportunities for teacher team leaders to arouse teachers' awareness of what unnoticed problems, such as a lack of methods reflecting a specific kind of core beliefs, might exist in their actual practices. This is especially important, as participant teacher team leaders (i.e., S, LY, and X) did not even align their own beliefs with their practices in the study. Reflection on these issues would likely benefit them on an individual and a professional level. I would suggest those teacher leaders identify and discuss these problems with their team members, and help provide solutions. For example, team leaders could facilitate discussion by asking all teachers in turn to prepare a presentation on student talk-centered teaching strategies. This would both encourage and model a less top-down model; the more experienced teachers would also gain new ideas to facilitate two-way conversation – a conversation instead of a lecture. The findings in this study suggested that more recent theories, or those currently studied in teacher education programs, are more likely to stick with and influence teachers in the long term. Thus, the new teachers coming out may have new ideas and teaching strategies to share that could even benefit the team leaders.

Moreover, I would suggest that teacher team leaders emphasize the importance of teacher reflection, especially between novice and experienced teachers. Teachers may reflect on their practices after class and then talk with peers about their reflections, perhaps to ask questions, gain insight, seek clarity, etc. In addition, I would also suggest teacher team leaders themselves engage in reflective practices, such as journaling, reviewing observations by other teachers, and exploring current research developments in both their core frameworks and those in their periphery. Teacher team leaders are also in-service teachers. Reflective practices help them acquire new knowledge, examine assumptions of everyday practice, and foster self-awareness and critical thinking (Boud et al., 1985; Boyd & Fales, 1983; Jarvis, 1992; Mezirow, 1981). By examining practices, teacher team leaders may see how reflective practices could alleviate tensions or inconsistencies between their beliefs and their practices and provide solutions to practical problems.

The last implication follows from my proposed CDST model. Based on the findings from the study, I proposed a conceptual model to explain the nexus of different constructs in the book and especially how the belief system of the reading teachers interacts and coadapts with their actual practice. Previous or existing models have different advantages and disadvantages, which overlap or compensate for each other in one way or another. However, all these modeling methods are deeply rooted or widely used in mathematical or psychological studies, with a great attempt to simulate the process of how a complex system runs. These modeling methods, while helpful and insightful, could not fit into this study on language teacher beliefs and practices. Therefore, I depicted and proposed the model using an interpretivist rather than a positivist approach. Mapping out the relationships among these studied constructs was thus not totally statistically guided but instead followed a meta-theoretical, conceptualized approach (Overton, 2013). Future research may refer to the model and make evidence-based adaptations.

7   Conclusion

This book reports that complexity was the primary feature of Chinese EFL teachers' belief systems. Quantitative findings from this study indicated that there was a significant association between reading beliefs and teaching beliefs only in the constructivist orientation, whereas there was no statistical association between reading beliefs and teaching beliefs in either behaviorist or cognitivist orientations. Findings from both within- and cross-case studies in the qualitative part also indicated how teachers' stated beliefs interacted with actual practices. By joining the existing literature, I discussed the findings of the study based on three research questions and provided different, possible explanations for this complex phenomenon. I also offered theoretical and practical implications for researchers, teachers, and teacher team leaders.

The completion of a book indicates a temporary stop of a project, but not of the journey. While my mentors, editors, and reviewers have provided me with insightful feedback, the book still has its limitations. For example, I was only able to present quantitative data to report interactions between reading beliefs and teaching beliefs in dominant orientations due to the limited time available. Also, I was unable to incorporate more literature into the literature review when compiling the book, as the amount of insightful articles and updated scholarship increases every month, even every day. However, I see these limitations as the way to improve or expand the line of inquiry. There is no end to learning.

References

Anderson, J. R. (1985). *Cognitive psychology and its implications*. W. H. Freeman.

Basturkmen, H., Loewen, S., & Ellis, R. (2004). Teachers' stated beliefs about incidental focus on form and their classroom practices. *Applied Linguistics, 25*(2), 243–272.

Borg, S. (2003). Teacher cognition in language teaching: A review of research into what language teachers think, know, believe and do. *Language Teaching, 36*(2), 81–109.

Borg, S. (2011). The impact of in-service education on language teachers' beliefs. *System, 39*(3), 370–380.

Boud, D., Keogh, R., & Walker, D. (1985). *Reflection: Turning experience into learning*. Kogan Page.

Boyd, E. M., & Fales, A. W. (1983). Reflective learning: Key to learning from experience. *Journal of Humanistic Psychology, 23*(2), 99–117.

Chai, C. S., Teo, T., & Lee, C. B. (2009). The change in epistemological beliefs and beliefs about teaching and learning: A study among pre-service teachers. *Asia-Pacific Journal of Teacher Education, 37*(4), 351–62. https://doi.org/10.1080/13598660903250381

Clark, C. A., Worthington, E. L., Jr., & Danser, D. B. (1988). The transmission of religious beliefs and practices from parents to firstborn early adolescent sons. *Journal of Marriage and the Family, 50*(2), 463–472. https://doi.org/10.2307/352011

Ertmer, P. A., & Newby, T. J. (2013). Behaviorism, cognitivism, constructivism: Comparing critical features from an instructional design perspective. *Performance Improvement Quarterly, 26*(2), 43–71.

Farrell, T. S. C. (1999). The reflective assignment: Unlocking pre-service English teachers' beliefs on grammar teaching. *RELC Journal, 30*(2).

Farrell, T. S. C., & Bennis, K. (2013). Reflecting on ESL teacher beliefs and classroom practices: A case study. *RELC Journal, 44*(2), 163–176.

Farrell, T. S. C., & Kun, S. T. K. (2007). Language policy, language teachers' beliefs, and classroom practices. *Applied Linguistics, 29*(3), 381–403.

Feryok, A. (2008). An Armenian English language teacher's practical theory of communicative language teaching. *System, 36*(2), 227–240.

Gao, Y. (2013). Incorporating sociocultural theory into second language (L2) reading instruction: A unit plan for EFL learners. *US-China Foreign Languages, 11*(11), 859–869.

Gao, Y. (2020). How transnational experiences and political, economic policies inform transnational intellectuals' identities and mobility: An autoethnographic study. *Higher Education Policy.* https://doi.org/10.1057/s41307-020-00187-w

Gao, Y., Fu, K., & Tao, X. (2021). How national and institutional policies facilitate academic resilience and e-learning in the unprecedented time? In M. E. Auer & D. Centea (Eds.), *Visions and concepts for education 4.0. ICBL 2020* (Advances in Intelligent Systems and Computing, Vol. 1314). Springer. https://doi.org/10.1007/978-3-030-67209-6_41

Garner, J., & Kaplan, A. (2019). A complex dynamic systems perspective on teacher learning and identity formation: an instrumental case. *Teachers and Teaching, 25*(1), 7–33. https://doi.org/10.1080/13540602.2018.1533811

Gatbonton, E. (2008). Looking beyond teachers' classroom behavior: Novice and experienced ESL teachers' pedagogical knowledge. *Language Teaching Research, 12*(2), 161–182.

Golombek, P. R. (1998). A study of language teachers' personal practical knowledge. *TESOL Quarterly, 32*(3), 447–464.

Gutierrez Almarza, G. (1996). Student foreign language teacher's knowledge growth. In D. Freeman & J. C. Richards (Eds.), *Teacher learning in language teaching* (pp. 50–78). Cambridge University Press.

Jarvis, P. (1992). Reflective practice and nursing. *Nurse Education Today, 12*(3), 174–181.

Johnson, K. E. (1992). The relationship between teachers' beliefs and practices during literacy instruction for non-native speakers of English. *Journal of Reading Behavior, 24*(1), 83–108.

Johnson, K. E. (1994). The emerging beliefs and instructional practices of pre-service ESL teachers. *Teaching and Teacher Education, 10*(4), 439–452.

Kaplan, A., & Garner, J. K. (2017). A complex dynamic systems approach on identity and its development: The dynamic systems model of role identity. *Developmental Psychology, 53*(11), 2036–2051.

Kaplan, A., & Garner, J. K. (2018). Teacher identity and motivation: The dynamic systems model of role identity. In P. Schutz, D. Cross Francis, & J. Hong (Eds.), *Research in teacher identity: Mapping challenges and innovations* (pp. 71–82). Springer.

Kırkgöz, Y. (2008). A case study of teachers' implementation of curriculum innovation in English language teaching in Turkish primary education. *Teaching and Teacher Education, 24*(7), 1859–1875.

Kitchener, R. F. (1986). *Piaget's theory of knowledge: Genetic epistemology & scientific reason.* Yale University Press.

Larsen-Freeman, D., & Cameron, L. (2008). Research methodology on language development from a complex systems perspective. *The Modern Language Journal, 92*(2), 200–213.

Li, C., & Ren, W. (2020). The complex dynamic systems theory and second language pragmatic development research. *Journal of Foreign Languages, 43*(3), 46–54.

Li, L. (2013). The complexity of language teachers' beliefs and practice: One EFL teacher's theories. *The Language Learning Journal, 41*(2), 175–191. https://doi.org/10.1080/09571736.2013.790132

Mezirow, J. (1981). A critical theory of adult learning and education. *Adult Education, 32*(1), 3–24.

Nespor, J. (1987). The role of beliefs in the practice of teaching. *Journal of Curriculum Studies, 19*(4), 317–328.

Ng, J., & Farrell, T. S. C. (2003). Do teachers' beliefs of grammar teaching match their classroom practices? A Singapore case study. In D. Derling, A. Q. Brown, & E. L. Low (Eds.), *English in Singapore: Research on grammar teaching* (pp. 128–137). McGraw Hill.

Nisbett, R. E., & Ross, L. (1980). *Human inference: Strategies and shortcomings of social judgment.* Prentice-Hall.

Orafi, S. M. S., & Borg, S. (2009). Intentions and realities in implementing communicative curriculum reform. *System, 37*(2), 243–253.

Overton, W. F. (2013). Relationism and relational developmental systems: A paradigm for developmental science in the post-Cartesian era. *Advances in Child Development and Behavior, 44*, 21–64.

Pajares, M. F. (1992). Teachers' beliefs and educational research: Cleaning up a messy construct. *Review of Educational Research, 62*(3), 307–332.

Patton, M. Q. (2002). *Qualitative research and evaluation methods* (3rd ed.). Sage.

Peterman, F. P. (1991, April 3). *An experienced teacher's emerging constructivist beliefs about teaching and learning* [Conference paper]. Annual Meeting of the American Educational Research Association, Chicago, IL, April 3–7, 1991.

Phipps, S., & Borg, S. (2009). Exploring tensions between teachers' grammar teaching beliefs and practices. *System, 37*(3), 380–390.

Plehn, K., Peterson, R. A., & Williams, D. (1998). Anxiety sensitivity: Its relationship to functional status in patients with chronic pain. *Journal Of Occupational Rehabilitation, 8,* 213–222.

Posner, G. J., Strike, K. A., Hewson, P. W., & Gertzog, W. A. (1982). Accommodation of a scientific conception: Toward a theory of conceptual change. *Science Education, 66*(2), 211–227.

Richardson, M. J., Dale, R., & Marsh, K. L. (2014). Complex dynamical systems in social and personality psychology: Theory, modeling, and analysis. In H. T. Reis & C. M. Judd (Eds.), *Handbook of research methods in social and personality psychology* (pp. 253–282). Cambridge University Press.

Skott, J. (2001). The emerging practices of a novice teacher: The roles of his school mathematics images. *Journal of Mathematics Teacher Education, 4*(1), 3–28.

Steenbeek, H., & van Geert, P. (2013). The emergence of learning-teaching trajectories in education: A complex dynamic systems approach. *Nonlinear Dynamics, Psychology, and Life Sciences, 17*(2), 233–267.

Stetsenko, A., & Vianna, E. (2009). Bridging developmental theory and educational practice: Lessons from the Vygotskian project. In O. A. Barbarin & B. H. Wasik (Eds.), *Handbook of child development and early education: Research to practice* (pp. 38–54). The Guilford Press.

Vygotsky, L. S. (1978). *Mind in society: The development of higher psychological processes.* Harvard University Press.

Zheng, H. (2013). Teachers' beliefs and practices: A dynamic and complex relationship. *Asia-Pacific Journal of Teacher Education, 41*(3), 331–343. https://doi.org/10.1080/1359866X.2013.809051

Zheng, H. (2015). *Teacher beliefs as a complex system: English language teachers in China.* Springer International. https://doi.org/10.1007/978-3-319-23009-2

Glossary

Actual practices   teachers' instructional practices of reading in the study. It is paired with stated beliefs, and the two constructs are the core constructs of the study.

Behaviorism   (also termed behavioral psychology) a theory of learning holding that all behaviors are acquired through conditioning.

Bottom-up model   defines reading from a language decoding perspective and believes that English reading means literally the mechanical process of going through materials or text printed or written in the English language.

Burke Reading Interview (BRI)   used to understand readers' beliefs about reading and influences on their past or current reading instructions.

Cognitivism   a response to the limitations of behaviorism. Cognitivism incorporates mental structures and processes into humans' learning. Cognitivists do not require an outward exhibition of knowledge but focus more on the internal processes and connections during learning.

Complex Dynamical System Theory (CDST)   a theory investigates the complex, non-linear, dynamical, self-organizing nature of a system or phenomenon. A system through a CDST perspective may include several subsystems that are co-adaptive and nested.

Constructivism   a theory of knowledge that argues that humans generate knowledge and meaning from an interaction between their experiences and their ideas.

Dominant belief   the phenomenon that while teachers may hold multiple beliefs, they always have one over the others in terms of the frequency or importance.

Dual beliefs   two competing beliefs that co-exist in teachers' belief system in the study. It may not be practical to figure out which one is more important between the two, as they may appear in different situations.

English as a foreign language (EFL)   English learning and teaching in a non-English-speaking region. It is sometimes interchangeably used as ESL (English as a second language), depending on a country's ideology or official recognition of the status of English. In China, while English is the foreign language with the largest number of people learning and speaking it, it is not officially a second language.

Exploratory sequential mixed-method design   technically, an exploratory sequential mixed-method study collects the qualitative data first, then present the quantitative data, and finally links the two together. In this study, while the first stage presented the data in a quantitative way, it collected all the qualitative data through open-ended questions.

Interactive model   combines both bottom-up and top-down models. Typical beliefs in this model argue good readers are both good decoders and good interpreters of the text. Therefore, the model strives to develop readers' skills and strategies in meaningful context.

Multiple beliefs   are referred to in the study specifically as three different beliefs in the teachers' belief system. Each type of the beliefs functions in a certain situation and may not be replaced or surpassed by the other two.

Paradigm shifts   the continuum of research paradigms from positivism (quantitative method-based) to pragmatism (mixed-methods-based), with other paradigms such as constructivism and transformativism in between. The continuum and shifts of the paradigms direct the development of studies.

Pragmatism   a research paradigm and worldview that explores, studies, and interprets real-world problems which are often complex, dynamic, and unstructured. The paradigm looks into what works in the world to construct and interpret the truth or knowledge, instead of what might be objectively defined as true or real. Interpretation in the paradigm is thus multidimensional and non-linear.

Reading beliefs   people's perceptions and understanding of what reading is about. They can relate to specific reading theories or reading models. For example, a person who regards reading as primarily a means to learn vocabulary and get information is usually a bottom-up reading predisposition.

Reading instruction   the practice of teaching reading.

Reading models   philosophical foundations that teachers use to direct their practices to teach language or literacy skills. Each reading model represents a certain reading philosophy. In this study, reading models include bottom-up, top-down, whole language approach, transactional, and complex dynamic system models.

Research paradigms   whole systems of thinking that direct established research traditions in a particular discipline (adapted from Neuman, 2011).

Stated beliefs   (also termed professed beliefs or written beliefs in the study) certain beliefs documented to reflect teachers' perceptions about a particular construct. In the study, stated beliefs about reading and teaching reading are documented.

Teacher team leaders   individuals (at most Chinese universities) who are responsible for organizing faculty meetings for teachers and evaluating teachers' practices. In the current study, S, LY, and X were all teacher team leaders. Different from teacher educators who are more on the educating side coaching teachers to acquire certain knowledge or practical skills, teacher team leaders are more on the supervising and administering side.

Teaching beliefs   the stated or professed beliefs about teaching or instructional process. In particular, it relates to the stated beliefs about teaching reading in this study.

Theoretical Orientations of Reading (TORP)   a survey developed by DeFord in 1978 when she originally completed her dissertation to explore reading teachers' theoretical orientations of reading. Generally, three reading orientations, i.e., behaviorism, cognitivism, and constructivism, were included in TORP. Each orientation represents a different way or philosophy to interpret reading. Different epistemological and ontological beliefs stand behind different reading orientations.

Top-down model   different from the bottom-up model which focuses on text, words, and materials, a top-down model by Ken Goodman focuses on the comprehension and information processing of the text, words, or materials. It is a model focusing on higher order mental instead of the physical text on the page. Therefore, *meaning* takes precedence over *structure*.

Transactional model   believes that both the reader and the text play important roles in the meaning formation process. In other words, meaning is formed by continuous transaction between the reader and the text.

Index

Printed in the United States
by Baker & Taylor Publisher Services